how to start a home-based

Business

how to start a home-based

Business

Bert Holtje and Susan Shelly

Guilford, Connecticut

Library of Congress Cataloging-in-Publication Data is available on file.

ISBN 978-0-7627-5946-0

Printed in the United States of America
10 9 8 7 6 5 4 3 2 1

Contents

Introduction:
Why a Home Based Business?

At some point in their careers, most people think about what it would be like to work for themselves and to work out of their homes. At first glance, the idea seems incredibly appealing. No more answering to a demanding boss. No more demanding schedules or taxing commutes. You could set your own hours and be there when the dog needs to go out or when the plumber comes to fix the drain. You wouldn't have to worry about what you were wearing, and you could finally get some decent coffee instead of the office sludge.

All of that sounds great, but even a little research quickly reveals that working for yourself isn't a walk in the park. If you think that starting and running a successful business from home is akin to a permanent vacation, you'd better give up the idea straightaway.

Running a home-based business does have many advantages. To be able to work in your own space, without the hassles of commuting and parking, is a very rewarding venture. But, it also requires a healthy dose of self discipline, business smarts, good organizational skills, and self motivation. You also need suitable working space within your home, knowledge of zoning and other legal issues associated with home businesses, the proper equipment and supplies, an understanding of tax considerations, and lots of other attributes in order to make your business a success.

More than twenty-four million Americans work in at-home businesses, according to the U.S. Small Business Administration (SBA), and 53 percent of all small businesses in the United States are run out of an owner's home. As the number of unemployed in the nation increased between the official beginning of the recession in December 2007 and 2009, the number of self-employed workers is expected to continue to increase.

If you're thinking of starting a home-based business, you'll need to consider a wide variety of issues, ranging from what business makes sense for you, to finding adequate work space, to letting others know about your business. You'll need the support of family and friends, enough capital to get started, a great business plan, and an optimistic outlook for your future. Running a business from home is great, but it involves some challenges. Your home office must function just as one would in an office building, which means that you may have to adjust your plans accordingly.

If you are just getting started, you will need to write a business plan, even if you aren't using borrowed capital. The tax implications for a home business are different than those for an office rented in an office building. Those who have yet to look deeply into the matter are initially thrilled that they might be able to write off some significant expenses by working from home. However, if you ever sell the home that houses you and your business, you may be hit with some taxes that you never planned for.

Far too many home-based entrepreneurs commingle their business money with their personal money when getting started. What should be a pretty simple tax return can turn into a nightmare when it comes time to separate the piles of invoices, bills, and checks that the local, state, and federal government want to tax.

And, speaking of money, how do you know how much to charge for your product or services? What are you worth? Don't ever make the mistake of charging less than someone providing a comparable service or product would just because your business is based in your home. Some people feel that their value must be diminished if they're not working out of a fancy office or have a storefront. The truth is, there are many businesses for which an office or storefront simply are not necessary, and home-based makes the most sense on many levels.

You'll need to learn how to screen clients and learn the essentials of providing good customer service to every customer. You'll need to consider the best record-keeping methods and be diligent about using those methods to help you keep your finances on track. You'll need to consider issues such as insurance and bonding, and figure out how to best market your home-based venture.

Regardless of what type of home-based business you're planning to start, taking the time to plan and prepare before you open your doors is critical, so give yourself a pat on the back for picking up this book. If you believe in your heart that having your own business and running it from your home is part of your life's plan, it just may be time to give it your best shot.

Now, let's get you started on *your* home-based business.

01 Considering a Home-Based Business

If you've always loved the thought of running your own business from home and are thinking that this might be the right time to get it going, you're preparing to join a diverse group of entrepreneurs running businesses ranging from pet sitting to electronic marketing.

We've all heard about people who have started businesses out of their homes that have turned out to be hugely successful. Bill Gates and Microsoft. Steve Jobs and Apple. Culinary queen and TV star Paula Deen launched her career in her own kitchen, making bag lunches. Mary Katherine Wagner's empire—Mary Kay Cosmetics—began with in-home demonstrations. All of these famous entrepreneurs had their own dreams, and they employed intelligence and determination to make them realities.

Remember, though, that for every Bill or Paula who has achieved fame and reached the pinnacle of his or her field, there are millions of thriving entrepreneurs you haven't heard of, happily operating businesses out of their homes. They won't ever be billionaires, perhaps not millionaires. They are, however, successfully living their dreams, and who can put a value on that?

Before you start working on your business plan, though, let's take a little time to consider the realities of starting your own home-based business. While you probably have all sorts of ideas running around in your head, starting your own business will require a significant degree of organization and preparation. Let's begin by considering a few questions. What exactly is an entrepreneur, and what are the qualities of a good one? Do you have the personality characteristics that are common to most successful entrepreneurs? What are the plusses and minuses of owning a home-based business? What are your motives for wanting to have your own home-based business? How about your qualifications? What are the different flavors of home businesses?

Is this the right time for you to start your own business? In short, are the cards on the table for you to make a home-based business venture work?

What Is an Entrepreneur?

The word "entrepreneur" comes from the French word "entreprende," which means "to undertake." An entrepreneur undertakes a business venture in anticipation of making profit. He or she plans, organizes, and operates the business.

There are, of course, many types of entrepreneurs who operate on many different levels. Some set up businesses in which they can work part time to supplement their family income. Others have retired from careers and are finally getting around to starting the business they've been thinking about for twenty-five years. Others are giving up working for somebody else and putting everything they've got into a business they hope will provide financially secure and comfortable lives for them and their families. Some people are lifelong entrepreneurs – the kind who start out buying candy and reselling it at a profit to other kids on the playground – while others come into entrepreneurship later in life. Regardless of what type of entrepreneur you are, be assured that you're in good company.

Qualities of a Successful Entrepreneur

You can find all sorts of lists informing you of the common characteristics of successful entrepreneurs. Which, though, are the ones that are really critical? John Sortino is a seasoned entrepreneur, having founded companies including the Vermont Teddy Bear Company, the largest manufacturer of handcrafted teddy bears in North America. Sortino, who is now in his 50s, started the teddy bear company from his Burlington, Vermont, home in 1981, as a young father who wanted to make a better toy for his son. Since then, he has launched the Chicago Bicycle Company, a manufacturer and assembler of cruiser/commuter-type bikes, and Plan B Technologies, Inc., a New York City-based computer security and support company. He also is the author of *The Complete Idiot's Guide to Being a Successful Entrepreneur*. Sortino's list of important qualities for a successful entrepreneur includes the following:

Good health and lots of energy. Starting and growing your own business requires putting in lots of long days (and often nights). An entrepreneur must be able to not only withstand physical and emotional stress, Sortino said, but to thrive on it. An entrepreneur should expect not to be sick. Emotional stability is critical, for you've got to be able to combat stress in both your business and your personal lives, and to keep moving ahead.

Self-Confidence. It's good to ask questions and be thoughtful and deliberate when making decisions, Sortino said, but once you've done your homework and decided on the path you want to take, being confident in your decision is crucial. Second guessing everything you do consumes time and energy, and can prevent your business from moving ahead. Projecting self-confidence is also assuring to customers, who expect you to be professional and in charge.

Leadership abilities. An entrepreneur must be an effective leader who is willing and able to take charge of situations. Effective entrepreneurs enjoy situations in which they are in control and have maximum authority. They usually don't work well in highly structured organizations in which they're expected to participate in business hierarchy. However, Sortino warned, being a leader is much different from being on a power trip, and good entrepreneurs enjoy controlling events and situations—not other people.

A let's-get-it-done attitude. Hand in hand with a high energy level is a sense of urgency to get things done and move ahead. It's this attitude that allows successful entrepreneurs to be self-motivated; to work long hours; and always be thinking of the next step, the next level. Many entrepreneurs lack the ability to be inactive, which can create challenges in their personal lives.

An understanding of the big picture. Starting your own home-based business will bring with it good days and bad days, Sortino advised, and it's very important to maintain a big-picture view when dealing with triumphs and failures. Running your own business is a constant series of ups and downs. Getting overly discouraged when something goes wrong, or overly confident when something goes right can get your business off track. You need to keep your eyes and mind on your long-term goals and look at the business in its entirety. An entrepreneur should be able to look at a situation clearly and hone in on the essence of what needs to be done.

A strong sense of reality. This applies both to the day-to-day operations of the business and in your outlook for the future, Sortino said. Keep track of what's going on so you have a clear picture of the business, and maintain a realistic view of what may lie ahead.

Attracted to challenges. Notice, said Sortino, that the attraction is to challenge, not to risk. "Of course there's risk involved with starting any business," Sortino said. "But, smart entrepreneurs have carefully calculated their risk and figured out whether or not it's a smart move to make. If it is, the risk turns into a challenge. If it's not, they'll stay away from it."

Ability to learn from mistakes. Nobody is perfect, and everybody will make mistakes. A good entrepreneur has the ability to recognize his mistakes, consider advice from others, learn from the mistakes, and move on to build his business. Business people who make the same mistakes over and over will find it difficult to keep moving ahead.

The ability to get along with others. You can have the best brain for business of anybody around, but if your personality turns off prospective customers, suppliers, and your employees, your business isn't going to be a success. Business dealings require a certain degree of emotional intelligence, which is being able to discern how others are feeling without them telling you, understanding how to talk to different people, and other personality skills.

The ability to recognize what you should do and what you should hire someone else to do. If your business genius is marketing, as is the case with Sortino, concentrate your efforts on marketing your business. If you absolutely hate keeping the books and it takes you eight hours to do what a good bookkeeper could do in two, hire the bookkeeper and go back to marketing your business.

A willingness to fail and keep going. Sortino strongly believes that failing in a business doesn't make you a failure. If your business fails, a smart entrepreneur assesses the situation, picks up the pieces, and moves on to try again, this time wiser and more savvy.

Other qualities thought to be common to successful entrepreneurs include: the ability to compromise, insightful, goal oriented, organized, persistent, dependable, perceptive, flexible, self motivated, able to express themselves verbally and in writing, a creative thinker, the ability to multi-task, an understanding of numbers, the ability to self promote, steady in a crisis, the ability to balance personal and business lives, and a willingness to ask for help when needed.

"Probably no one has all of these qualities, but if you're looking at the list and don't recognize yourself at all, you might want to reconsider whether starting your own business is the right thing for you," Sortino said. "If you see yourself all over that list, chances are you've got the qualities it takes to be a successful entrepreneur."

More Qualities of a Successful Entrepreneur

- The ability to cooperate with people you might disagree with
- The ability to manage your own time effectively and to see that your colleagues don't waste their time
- The ability to make decisions based on facts, not emotions, and the ability to enforce them without getting personal
- The ability to make schedules, adhere to them, and ensure that others don't drop the ball
- The ability to manage complex details and to direct the work of others who are responsible for any of the tasks
- The ability to set your own goals and the goals of others involved in a project
- The ability to accept responsibility and to delegate it to others
- The ability to graciously accept responsibility for failure as well as success

Advantages and Disadvantages of a Home-Based Business

There's some irony in the fact that, often, the advantages and disadvantages of operating a business from your home can become blurred. It might seem like a huge advantage on some days to be able to put work aside and make lunch for your seven-year-old, while on other days it's a huge disadvantage to be forced to put work aside and make lunch because you need to finish a job for a client by 3 o'clock that very afternoon. Some at-home entrepreneurs get lonely after a while and miss the camaraderie that occurs in a business setting. Others find out they're not as disciplined as they'd thought and have trouble staying on task. As with any job, running a home-based business isn't perfect. Let's have a look at some of the advantages and disadvantages.

Advantages

It's less expensive than renting space. You need much less cash to set up a business at home than you would to get started out of an office or other business space, where you'd need to think about deposits, monthly rent, and so forth. You probably have a desk or something that can serve as workspace at home, while if you were setting up an office elsewhere you'd have to buy furniture and equipment, in addition to leasing the space.

It's an easy commute. If you've ever spent an hour on the road every day getting back and forth to work—and many people spend a lot more time than that—you surely can appreciate this huge advantage of working from home. Think about this. According to the U.S. Federal Highway Administration, the average American worker spends 348 hours a year getting back and forth to work. That's nearly 30 hours a month, or almost eight hours a week. Operating a home-based business doesn't mean that you'll never need to drive again, but it sure cuts down on driving time and frees you up for other things. And, letting the car or truck sit more means fewer expenses for gas, tolls, and upkeep.

You're in charge of your own schedule. No longer do you have to rush out of work to keep that last appointment of the day with your dentist, or take time off work to wait for the cable guy to show up. Working at home often means that you can make your own schedule, as long as you also make sure you finish all the work that needs to be completed. Many people who run businesses out of their homes will take breaks to exercise, drive a kid someplace, take an elderly neighbor to an appointment, or engage in other activities. You can take advantage of your body clock by starting your work at 6 A.M. when you're at your best, or working into the wee hours, if that's your style. And, if you're a parent and your child is sick, it's a real comfort to be at home to keep an eye on her.

You keep the money you make. Sure, you have to meet your expenses and pay your taxes, but, when you're running your own business, the money left over at the end of the day belongs to you, not an employer or company. A graphic designer working in an agency, for instance, might earn $28 an hour, while her employer charges the client $60 an hour for her work. The same designer working on her own can charge —and keep—the $60 an hour.

There are tax advantages associated with a home business. You get to deduct part of the operating and depreciation expenses on your home, including your mortgage, insurance, property taxes, utilities, and maintenance, as business expenses. You'll read more about that in chapter 9.

You get to wear a lot of hats. Think of it. You get to be the CEO, marketing professional, customer service representative, bill collector, sales director, business development manager, and custodian, all within your own business! These opportunities, of course, pave the way for professional development and growth.

You can focus your energies on the important parts of your business. No more interoffice memos about keeping the coffee room clean or employees who are taking longer than permitted lunch breaks. No more pointless meetings, meetings to plan future meetings, or interoffice politics. You get to decide what's important and how you'll spend the hours of your day.

Disadvantages

You're in charge of your own schedule. You're right, this was listed under advantages, too. Being in charge of your own schedule can be a good news/bad news item, depending on your ability to manage your time and stay on task. While it's great to be able to take a little time off to get your child to the doctor or meet with your accountant, it's probably not so great to be taking time off every morning to watch "The View."

You get to wear a lot of hats. Yes, this one also was listed under advantages. While serving in a variety of capacities can help you to grow professionally, it also can be draining and create a situation where you're trying to do so much that you're not doing anything particularly well.

It's all on you. Many municipalities have zoning restrictions and other laws that affect home-based businesses. If it's your business, it's on you to check on zoning and other legal issues that may limit the types of businesses you're able to have, the number of employees, and so on. Also, you'll need to find out if you need permits, business licenses, registrations, and so forth. This also applies to tax and other financial regulations.

You'll need to manage the expectations of others. Many people assume that people who work at home enjoy extremely flexible schedules that allow them to be available on a moment's notice to help with a project at school, drive a neighbor to an appointment, or serve as the neighborhood coordinator for the American Heart Association's fundraising drive. While managing your own schedule can be a real advantage, you'll need to stand firm and not let others infringe on your time. Remember that very few people would ask you to leave your office to drive them to an appointment.

You may find yourself conflicted between your work and family obligations. It's easy for the lines to blur when you're working and living in the same place, and many an entrepreneur has experienced tension over keeping the family happy while keeping up with the demands of the business, especially when it's just getting started.

The Different Flavors of Home-Based Businesses

There are several basic types of home-based businesses. Once you figure out which of them you're best suited to, you can begin to narrow down your business choice.

Home-based franchise. Most people probably think of burgers or pizza when they hear the word franchise, but the truth is, there are many types of franchises that can be run from home, including janitorial services, health care, children's products and services, recreation, and secretarial and financial services. The cost of a franchise can range from less than $10,000 to five million dollars or more, depending on the type of franchise, location, size, and other factors.

Service-based business. People have made successful businesses selling services ranging from child care to financial consulting, with an almost seemingly endless list of possibilities. As your business grows, you might consider hiring others to provide the same services, or branching out with additional services. The types of services you're able to sell will vary depending on your location, the competition, and other factors.

Product-based business. Obviously, a product-based business sells products instead of services. Internet sales have made it completely feasible to run product-based businesses from home, because you don't need to stock a great deal of inventory. You might sell a product that you buy from a third party, or you might manufacture and sell the product yourself. As with a service-based business, you'll need to have sales skills, along with business knowledge.

What Specific Business Should You Consider?

You probably wouldn't have picked up this book if you didn't have at least an idea or two of what type of business you're interested in starting. Once you've considered whether you're looking at a home-based franchise, a service-based business, product-based or business to business, you'll have to narrow down your choice to a specific product or service that you'll provide. Once you've come up with an idea, the question becomes, how do you know if it's a good one, and how do you know if it's right for you? There is no end to advice available on this topic, but basically, when you're thinking about starting your own at-home business, you'll need to consider the following:

- What do you love to do?
- What do you do well?
- What sort of job suits your lifestyle?
- How much money do you aspire to earn?
- How much money do you have, or can you get for your start-up?
- What sort of job training and/or experience do you have?
- Is there a market for your product or services?
- How much competition is there in the business you're considering?

If you're thinking about starting your own home-based business, it may be that you're looking to do something different than your current job, assuming that you're employed. Often, the temptation is to head out on your own and do the same sort of work you've been doing at your place of employment. And, that can turn out just fine, assuming that you really like what you do. If you're not happy with the work you do for an employer, however, ask yourself it you'll be any happier doing it on your own.

Some lucky people are able to parlay their hobbies into money-making ventures, such as arranging tours for bicyclists, restoring old cars, or baking and decorating cakes for special occasions. If there's something that you love and can do well enough that other people are willing to pay you for it, you might just be able to turn a hobby into a job. There are hundreds of stories of entrepreneurs who have launched hobby-based businesses ranging from organizing shopping tours in cities around the world, to planning parties for clients, to making and delivering meals for working parents who don't have time to cook.

Your previous job and life experience also should factor into the type of business you decide to pursue. If you decide you'd like to start up a marketing consultant business, but you have no marketing training or experience, chances are you'll have a very short client list. If you've left a career of teaching to start a business tutoring high school students preparing to take the SAT exam, on the other hand, you may find you're forced to turn down potential customers.

And, while considering your professional and life experience, also consider your current lifestyle and the type of lifestyle you aspire to. A mom with four school-age children might want to consider a different type of at-home business than a woman who has no child responsibilities. That's not to imply that the mom's business can't be just as successful and rewarding, but she may want to think about one that fits into her busy lifestyle, perhaps even one in which her children can be involved.

If you're looking for a business that produces a full-time income for you, or you and your family, you'll need to think differently about your start-up than someone looking to earn some supplemental income or pad the retirement nest a bit.

To get an idea of what you need to earn (which is very different than what you want to earn), you need to figure out your living costs and what your business costs will look like. Consider factors such as equipment you might need to buy, the need to buy your own health insurance, tax considerations, and so forth, and add those costs to your living costs. The cost of starting an at-home business varies tremendously, depending on the type and scope of the business. You can start a business such as a cleaning service or dog sitting business for a couple of hundred dollars, or you can spend tens of thousands of dollars for a business that requires you to stock a lot of inventory and involves high expenses.

Don't be discouraged if you have limited start-up money available. Entrepreneur. com lists fifty-five home-based businesses with start-up costs of $5,000 or less. These businesses include cleaning service, computer repair, consulting, e-bay assistance, landscaping, rug cleaning, web designer, photographer, gift baskets, bed and break-fast, and a Christmas tree farm, with lots of other suggestions. You can check it out at www.entrepreneur.com/homebasedbiz/homebasedideas/article201588-5.html.

Other low cost start-ups include: tutoring, hair care/makeup, child care provider, catering, online professor, financial services consultant, party planning, computer services, and personal organizer.

Because almost all new businesses experience lag periods as they establish their customer bases and get off the ground, you should have enough money to support yourself for at least a year as you get your business established. Many business experts recommend that you're covered for 18 to 24 months. That money can come from your savings, from another wage earner in the family, or in loans from individuals or institutions. You'll need it to support yourself, any dependents, and your business until you begin to realize a profit. Obtaining that money, or at least commitments for that money, is imperative before you move ahead.

You may have firmly decided what type of home-based business you want to have a long time ago. If so, you'll need to consider the financial aspects associated with it, along with how a home-based business will fit your lifestyle and the lives of others with whom you share your home.

You'll also need to research the market in which you'll be operating and learn who your competitors are. Market research sounds complicated, but it's actually nothing more than gathering and analyzing information that helps you understand who and where your potential customers are, and how you can effectively market your goods or services to them. You can do this by talking to potential customers about their wants and needs, being attentive to how and where your competitors advertise, and asking for advice from any associations or organizations that may be able to help you.

Take a Look at Your Timing

In the midst of the worst economic crisis since the Great Depression, your friends and family may let you know they think you've lost it should you happen to mention at the next cookout or family dinner that you're planning to start up a home-based business. Don't worry. You can come right back at them with these fun facts:

- More than half of the 30 corporations that make up the Dow Jones Industrial Average were started during recessions.
- Hewlett-Packard got its start during the Great Depression.
- The Disney start-up was during the recession of 1923–24.
- Bill Gates kicked off Microsoft during the recession of 1975.

Of course, you should be mindful of the business climate when considering what type of business to start. You want to find a business that actually uses the (good or bad) economy in its favor, such as a claims service, repair service for big-ticket items such as computers or TVs, secretarial or bookkeeping service for small businesses looking to outsource work, job interview coach, and resume writing.

Frequently Asked Questions

1. *With so many people already operating home-based businesses, or looking to start one, do I stand a chance?*
   The truth is that many small businesses fail. However, that is usually because the person or people behind them didn't take the time and effort necessary to get everything in order before they started doing business. Many business hopefuls do not even bother to write a business plan, which is like heading out on a cross-country road trip without a GPS or even a map. You have a very good chance of becoming a successful entrepreneur if you are smart, diligent, and willing to work hard to get your business up and running.

2. *How do I know what's the best type of home-based business for me?*
   When deciding what type of business you'll start, you need to consider your interests, abilities, and experience. If you live to bake fancy cakes, a cake baking and decorating business might be the perfect business. That is, of course, once you confirm there's a market for such a business in your area. If you've worked in the insurance industry for years, perhaps a consulting job is in your future.

02

Getting Started I: The Legalities

It would be nice to be able to skate over the legalities of starting a home-based business and just get on with it. Unfortunately, that's not a good plan, because that attitude can land you in trouble and derail your business before it ever gets off the ground.

If, after much thought, deliberation, and planning, you've decided on the type of business you want to start, you've determined that there's a viable market for such a business, and you're confident that you're in a financial position to give it a try, it's time to start considering the legalities involved with your venture.

The first thing you'll need to decide is what kind of business you're going to be.

What Kind of Business Am I?

What kind of business you're going to be, in this instance, doesn't refer to whether your business is a service or product-based company, or if you're looking into buying a Dunkin' Donuts franchise. Asking what kind of business you'll open refers to the structure of the business—how your business will be organized and incorporated. There are three basic types of business organizational structures: sole proprietorships, partnerships, and corporations. Let's have a look at what each type is, and the legal implications it could have for your business.

Sole Proprietorships

A sole proprietorship is the most common type of business and the most hassle free to get up and running. Many people, in fact, operate sole proprietorships without even realizing it. The woman who watches your neighbor's

Think carefully about consulting with a good business lawyer when you're figuring out what type of business to set up. No, you don't necessarily need a lawyer, but having one will help assure that you've covered all your bases and you're within the legal guidelines to which you must adhere.

twins every day is a sole proprietor. The husband and wife who do the gardening work for your mother are sole proprietors, too, as is the woman at your church who offers piano and voice lessons for a good portion of kids in the congregation.

Anyone who offers services or products to others and hasn't established herself as a different kind of business entity is a sole proprietor.

Sole proprietorships are extremely popular because they're easy and inexpensive to start, and any profits from the business go directly to the owner. In addition, according to the Small Business Administration, the average 13.3 percent tax rate of sole proprietorships is lower than the average rates of partnerships (23.6 percent) or corporations (26.9 percent).

As a sole proprietor, you don't have to pay corporate taxes. Your taxes come out of your income, all of which is taxable. You get to deduct your business expenses, which is a good thing. You are responsible for complying with licensing requirements in your state, as well as with local regulations and zoning laws.

While we say that those entrepreneurs who operate sole proprietorships are in business on their own, or own their own businesses, the truth is that it's very difficult to be in business on your own.

It's just about impossible to be in business by yourself. You might think you're going to be, and others might perceive that you're in business by yourself, but really, it can't happen.

If you've gotten funding for your business from any source, then you're in business with that funding source. Whether it's the bank, or your Uncle Herb, or whomever, if you've borrowed money to finance your venture, you can't truly be in business by and for yourself.

Regardless of what type of business you have, you're in business with, and for, the government. Government regulations dictate to some degree how you'll run your business, and the government is happy to share any money you make through your business.

If your business has a board of directors or shareholders, you're not flying solo. You might be the boss, or you might run the business, but you're really not in it alone. You can, however, be the sole proprietor of a business, which means you get to be completely responsible for all business conducted, and have total control of the business.

While there are many advantages to having a sole proprietorship, there's one serious disadvantage. The downside is that, as a sole proprietor, you personally assume all of the liabilities of the business. You're not separate from your business, meaning that if you get sued, you are responsible. Any legal or financial obligations of the business get passed directly to you, the sole proprietor, and you're responsible for making good on them. Sole proprietorships may have employees, but the owner is responsible for any claims made against the business because of something an employee did.

In our lawsuit-happy society, one major claim could wipe out years of hard work and profits. If your business is one with a high risk of liability, a sole proprietorship probably isn't your best choice of structure. Regardless of what type of business you're starting, if you choose the sole proprietorship form of ownership, be sure to talk to a good insurance person, lawyer, or dependable businessperson about liability and insurance issues. Some types of insurance are much better for sole proprietorships than others, and you've got to get the best coverage you can in the event that something happens.

Despite that rather sobering drawback to this form of business, however, the majority of small businesses in the United States operate as sole proprietorships.

Let's take a closer look at why they're so popular.

- It's easy. A sole proprietorship is the easiest legal structure to get started. All you have to do is apply for an occupational business license in the community or municipality within which the business will be located, and file any fictitious names.
- It's fast. You usually can get a license very soon after applying for it, and you're free to open your business. There's not much waiting for approval or messing around with red tape involved with a sole proprietorship.
- It's streamlined. If you're in business by yourself, with no employees, you can use your social security number as your taxpayer identification number. If you have employees, you need to request an employer identification number from the IRS.

- There may be tax advantages. When you're first starting up a sole proprietorship, there usually are some tax advantages that you can take, personally. Remember, that for tax purposes, the IRS treats you and your business as one. You might see some savings, due to investment tax credits.

On the other hand, however, there are some troubling aspects associated with sole proprietorships, in addition to the big drawback associated with liability. Let's take a closer look at those.

- You need to rely solely on your own expertise. That might not be a bad thing, if you're an expert at whatever you're doing. Just remember, however, that there are many aspects of running a business, and nobody is an expert at all of them. Don't be afraid to ask for help for help in the areas where you are not an expert.
- You need to rely on your own assets. If you borrow $100,000 from the bank, the collateral on that loan will depend solely on your assets. If you invest your own money in the business, it probably won't be as much as you could have raised if you had a partner or two. The fact is, the more money of your own you have to put into your business, the more money you'll probably be able to get from a lender. A bank is a lot more likely to lend you $100,000 for your business if you've put $100,000 into it.
- Your business will no longer exist if you become disabled or die. That can cause some real problems when it comes time to dispose of the business, divide the estate, and so forth.
- A sole proprietor loses out on some tax breaks that a corporation gets, such as deductions for insurance expenses and health benefits.

Partnerships

A good business partnership can be nearly as great and satisfying as a good personal partnership. On the flip side, a bad business partnership can be nearly as lousy as a bad personal relationship. There are a couple of types of partnerships, but basically, a business partnership occurs when two or more people agree to work together in one business that has not been incorporated.

If you're thinking about going into business with a partner, conduct an assessment of the person's work style, work ethic, personal traits, and strengths and weaknesses. If you don't know the person well enough to make those assessments, you probably don't know each other well enough to be business partners.

Business partnerships require all partners to be on the same page regarding how the business will be run, its goals, and the guiding principles that will lead the business. Business philosophy is an important aspect of being a business owner, and partners who don't share a similar business philosophy often run into serious problems. Partnerships should be clearly defined and all expectations set to paper before the business opens. You'll need to have all parties sign a partnership agreement before your business gets going.

On a practical note pertaining to a home-based business, how will you and your partner or partners decide from whose home the business should be run? While there are many things to be considered regarding compatibility, philosophy, and expectations, there also are some legal implications associated with business partnerships.

In a general partnership, the partners are jointly responsible for the business' debts and liabilities. Partners can agree among themselves how they will share the profits and losses of the business, but as far as the law is concerned, each one is equally responsible for the business. That's why it's really important to get into writing who is responsible for what, and how profits and losses will be divided. A business partnership isn't taxed as a business; its partners are taxed as individuals on their incomes and can deduct business expenses as individuals.

Entrepreneurs sometimes take on partners solely because they need money, and it often leads to trouble. If the only reason you want a partner is because she'll bring capital to your venture, then you need an investor, or a limited partner, but not a general partner. Be careful you don't confuse these things. You might end up with a partner whom you'll resent, because she wants (rightly so) to be involved with running what you consider your business. A general partner shares more than financing.

Business Warning

You can get business partnership forms in a business supply store or online that you can fill out yourselves, but it's highly advisable to get a lawyer to work with you on a partnership agreement. Not only does it cover your butt down the road, but it helps to get everyone on the same page regarding expectations and responsibilities.

In a limited liability partnership, a limited liability partner is responsible only for the investment that he's made in the company. Usually, a limited liability partner invests in the company, but isn't directly involved with the day to day operations, which are left to the general partner. Limited liability partnerships have to be formed through a filing with the state, and a filing and yearly fees apply. While there are some advantages to limited liability partnerships, they aren't trouble free.

Let's take a look at some advantages and disadvantages of business partnerships. Advantages include:

- Having a partner means you're sharing the liability associated with the business. You and your partner are still responsible, but at least it's a shared responsibility.
- Partners' strengths can compensate for one another's weaknesses. If one of you is a great salesperson, and the other is great at creating new products, you will complement each other when the business gets underway. The flip side, of course, is that if both of you are great salespeople, but are terrible at business management, you're going to be looking at a problem when it comes time to run the business.
- Partnerships generally can generate more funding than sole proprietorships. Because there are two or more of you, you've often got more in the way of assets than just one person would. Investors often are more willing to give money to a partnership than a sole proprietorship.
- If one partner dies or becomes disabled, the business can continue. Unlike with a sole proprietorship, the remaining partner or partners can keep the business up and running.
- It can be a lot of fun to work with a partner whom you get along with really well. Working alone isn't for everyone, and many people find that having a partner makes their work much more enjoyable, as well as providing someone with whom to share ideas and plans.

Some disadvantages of partnerships include the following:

- When you're in business you always have responsibilities to attend to, but, when you're in business with partners, you have to be accountable to one another all the time. Common courtesy and good business sense dictates that you check with your partner before you go out of town, leave work early to go golfing, or okay the purchase of new equipment. Some people enjoy talking things over and working as a team, but others prefer to be free to make decisions on their own.

- You have to share control of the business. Some people have trouble sharing the control, especially if the business was their idea. Think about whether you're willing to do that, before you take on a partner. If you've already started the business and are thinking of getting a partner, think even harder. Your partner is sure to have opinions and input, and you may have to make a lot of changes.

- You have to share the wealth. Having a partner means sharing the profits. Hopefully, your partnership will generate more profits than you would have on your own, and you'll end up better off. But, you won't be in a take-all situation.

Corporations

Corporations have distinct advantages over other business structures in that they offer some protection from liability to individuals. However, they are more complicated to set up and run because they are legally formed business structures and must comply with applicable laws and regulations.

While larger businesses typically are run as corporations, even a small business of one or two people can incorporate. Corporations are comprised of shareholders, who are the owners; a board of directors, elected by the shareholders to manage the corporation; and officers who handle the day-to-day running of the business. It varies from state to state, but in some cases, the business owner can be the only shareholder, serve as the board of directors, and hold all the positions of officers. Talk about responsibility!

When tax season rolls around, the corporation pays on the profits it generated that year and then divides the profits among the shareholders.

Definition

A corporation made up of just a few people, and often just one person, is called a close corporation. It's privately owned and serves to separate the assets and liabilities of the business from those of the owner.

As stated, the big advantage of incorporating your business is that it separates the business responsibilities from your personal responsibilities and allows you to protect your personal assets in the event of a lawsuit. It also enables you to leave the business and have the business continue to operate, as you and the business are separate.

Forming a corporation must be done according to laws of your state. There are various fees involved, and you'll need to get a lawyer to assist you. Many businesses begin as sole proprietorships or partnerships, and incorporate after they've experienced some significant growth. Some people feel that setting up a corporation is just too complicated for a small business, which is a definite downside. However, before you decide, consider some pros and cons of the corporate structure of ownership.

Advantages include:

- It can be easier to raise start-up capital as a corporation. You can sell stock privately, and may not have to seek money from banks and other commercial sources. Keep in mind, however, that whether or not you are incorporated, banks and other lending institutions take the same view of your ability to repay as will most other sources.
- Your tax rate may be lower, but this may come at a price. Your accountant can tell you why when he or she has the complete picture.
- It's generally easier to transfer ownership in a corporation than it is with other forms of organization. You can sell your corporate stock, but you have nothing to sell as a partnership. A partnership must be dissolved and re-established if it is to pass to others.
- You can set up more fringe benefits for yourself under a corporate structure than you might be able to under any of the other forms.
- If you have employees and any of them causes the corporation to be sued, you are better insulated from the suit than you might be under any other form.
- If growth beyond a one-person consultancy is in your plan, it's easier to attract good employees to a company structured as a corporation than any other form. Stock ownership is a tempting carrot for many people.
- There are many estate planning benefits available that are not available to other forms.
- If there is even the slightest hint that your partners might be contentious, the corporation is the best way to go. A parting of the ways doesn't involve dissolution of a corporation as it does with a partnership.

As attractive as the corporate structure can be, a few downside issues must be considered. Chief among these problems are:

■ There is far more paperwork required to operate a corporation than any of the other forms. The records that you are legally obliged to keep can wear you down very quickly.

■ It does cost more to operate as a corporation than it does to operate any of the other forms. Accounting fees are higher, mainly because of the amount of documentation the various taxing authorities require. The legal fees to incorporate will be higher, too.

■ A corporation is required to pay taxes on its profits before it distributes dividends to stockholders who must also pay taxes on the money they receive. It's not exactly double taxation, but the amounts can eat into what you thought should be yours. There are legal ways to make sure that this isn't a big problem, but the legal and accounting advice needed to help you maximize your personal income will be costly. If you think that bumping up your salary might eliminate the profits on which your corporation might have to pay taxes, forget about it. The IRS is permitted to set salary levels and dividends if it sees evidence of this ploy.

■ As a sole proprietor you can run your business from your personal checkbook. But as a corporation, if you make a payment on a personally owned car from your corporate checkbook, you will be in trouble.

Regardless of what type of business you decide you'll be, get as much information as you can regarding the legal and financial implications. Remember that too much information is better than not enough when it comes to protecting you and your family.

Choosing and Registering a Name for Your Company

While it seems like choosing a name for your company should be fun, for many entrepreneurs it's one of the hardest parts of getting a business up and running. This is, I think, because the name of your business is so public. You can do a lot of work behind the scenes, but once you hoist a sign with your business name on it you're putting it out there for everybody to see and talk about.

And, in addition to the stress of picking exactly the right name for your business, you need to be sure that you don't choose a name that's already taken (or very close to one already taken), that your name is in accordance with any state or local regulations, and that it is in accord with the type of business structure you've chosen for your company.

As far as choosing a name that will get people to notice your business, keep the following tips in mind:

- The name should be easy to pronounce and spell.
- It should be short so people can remember it.
- It should be original.
- It should tell what your company is or does.
- It should convey something positive about your company.

All you have to do is pick up a copy of your phone book and turn to the Yellow Pages to see examples of some really good and really not-so-good business names. *Meb Consulting* is short and tells me that it's a consulting business, but there are lots of different kinds of consultants. *Business Link* clues me in that it's a business-related company, but it doesn't tell me that it's actually a copying and duplicating service. *Hettinger Painting, Faux Finishing, Murals, & Fine Art* tells me everything (and more) than I really need to know, but how am I going to remember it?

On the other hand, *Laurel Street Complete Recycling Center* tells me not only what the business is, but where it is, as well. *Hobbie Horse Daycare Center* informs of the type of business and creates a pleasant image in my mind. *Stone Creek Excavating* defines the business while portraying an image of strength and toughness—the ability to get the job done.

Some business owners hire a marketing firm or advertising agency to help them name their businesses. If you're tempted to do that, be sure you pay attention to the name of the firm that you hire. If it's not inspiring, chances are that the name the firm comes up with for you won't be either.

Remember that the name you choose can't be misleading, or misrepresent your qualifications. You can't name your business *Cornerstone Licensed Counseling Services*, for instance, if you're not a licensed counselor or have other licensed counselors on staff. Your name can not imply that your business is something that it's not.

If your business is a sole proprietorship, it's assumed that it will operate under your name. If you're a sole proprietor and want to create or change the name of the business, you'd need to file a fictitious name statement, sometimes called a doing business as (d/b/a) form. This gives you the legal right to the name of your business within the jurisdiction of the governing body with which the statement was filed. Usually, this is done on a county level, so no one else within your county can have a business with the same name as yours.

The same pretty much goes for a partnership. It's assumed that the business will operate under the names of the partners. If they choose to name it something else, they'll need to get a fictitious owner affidavit, which usually gets filed with the county's recorder of deeds.

The name of a limited liability partnership, though, has to be filed with the state, and must indicate that the business is a limited liability partnership either by including that phrase, or the initials L.L.P. or in some other way, as directed by the state.

As with a limited liability partnership, the name of a corporation needs to be registered with the state, and it must indicate that the business is incorporated by including the word "corporation," "incorporated," "limited," or "company." Sometimes an abbreviation like "Inc.," "Ltd." or "Co." can be used, depending on your state's specifications. The name of a corporation should be filed at the same time the business files to become a corporation. If another business already has the name you choose, you'll need to pick another one.

So, you see, choosing a name for your business isn't something to be done without significant thought and planning. It's usually good to run the name you're thinking about by some friends or family members before you commit to it. And, be sure to spend some time with the name before you make it official.

Applying for a Business License

Licensing requirements will vary, depending on where you live, so it's important that you do your homework and find out what is required of you. Your business actually could fall under the requirements of several jurisdictions, such as local and state. It also may be regulated by the industry you're in. If you're starting your own CPA business, for instance, you need to be licensed as a CPA – you can't just declare yourself to be one, even if you have significant experience in the accounting field. The same goes for financial brokers, doctors, dentists, veterinarians, insurance brokers, licensed counselors, and so on. If you're in a field that requires licensing, it's almost certain that you know that and have adhered to the requirements. If you're uncertain, however, check out the Web site of a professional organization in your field and make sure.

To find out what type or types of licenses you'll need, start by contacting local officials. This might be your town or city hall, township building, or other sort of municipal headquarters. If you're unsure, check the blue pages in your telephone book or do an online search on the Web site of the municipality in which you reside.

A word to the wise is, before applying for a business license, be sure you have all your ducks in row. When you apply for a business license, it can begin a chain reaction. You may need to have zoning approval before you can get a business license or health department approvals if your business involves food. In some cities, you might even need approval from the arts commission before you put out a sign or erect an awning.

A great place to start when trying to figure out what sorts of licenses you need is your local chamber of commerce. Chambers are great resources for businesspeople. The Small Business Administration also offers useful information in the form of a state-by-state list of Web sites that contain licensing information. Check that out at www.sba.gov/hotlist/license.html.

Additionally, you could contact the applicable bureau in your state's Department of State, the Department of Consumer Affairs, your local records bureau, or another agency that provides information about business licenses.

Getting a business license shouldn't be a problem, but you need to be sure to cover your bases. Opening a business without the proper licenses is highly unadvisable, as it can result in your business being shut down just as it's getting off the ground. Even a temporary shutdown can be costly, and sends a very negative message to customers and potential customers. Also, remember that business licenses need to be renewed at regular intervals. Be sure to keep good records so you're not surprised when a renewal is due.

Setting Up a Business Bank Account and Getting to Know Your Bankers

Finding the right bank and establishing the right kind of business account will be important to the future of your business. Sure, you can always change to another bank, but establishing a good relationship from the start will provide many advantages.

The first mistake you want to avoid is turning to the banks you use for your personal accounts without doing any research at all. Sure, the temptation is to go with what you know, but while a small savings and loan bank may know the home mortgage business inside and out, it might not have a clue about your business. The closer you live to large, metropolitan areas, the wider your choice of banks will be. However, unless you need regular face-to-face contact with your banker, it's possible to do your banking almost anywhere over the Internet.

Probably the best way to begin your search for the bank that's right for you is to talk with other small business owners and get their views on the service they have experienced. That's just the first step; your next task is to determine whether your type of small business is something that the bank you approach understands.

Your banker should have a variety of different business banking programs from which you can choose. A creative banker will show you how he or she can put together a banking program that addresses your specific needs if none of the bank's off-the-shelf programs provides a good enough fit.

Be sure to ask if the bank participates in the Small Business Administration's government guaranteed loan program—and make sure that your business will qualify for participation in the program if you plan to seek finances from them.

There is hardly a bank today that doesn't have some sort of online banking program. You may want all of your clients' checks to be sent directly to your bank, but you should be notified by the bank electronically when each check clears. You don't want to send a nasty letter to a client who has sent a check to your bank which the bank has yet to clear.

Check for any special start-up programs, such as special interest rates on small business loans. Ask about night depository if your business is one that will require you to deposit cash receipts after banking hours.

Also, ask about interest-bearing accounts and what the bank wants from you in return for the interest. You may want a combination checking and savings account. Ask about the credit and debit cards the bank has available for commercial accounts, and be sure to get the minimum balance levels for all the accounts the banker discusses with you.

If a bank also offers financial brokerage accounts, discuss these services, too. If you are going to park money from time to time, it probably doesn't make sense to leave it in a general bank savings account. See what they offer that provides a higher interest rate, but be sure to understand all the restrictions that are placed in the investment. If you need cash in a hurry, some of these high interest rate instruments will not be for you.

Banks are famous for merging, purging, coming, and going. The economy we're in is not a stable time for banks, or for any other financial institutions, for that matter. The Federal Deposit Insurance Corporation has raised the limit on deposits it will insure, and the honchos at banks we used to revere are being called by less than flattering names. All this makes it even more difficult to select a bank for your business, and means that you should learn as much as you can about the banks you are considering.

Other Professionals to Look For

Your bankers, including loan officers, will be very important to the future of your business. You also should establish relationships with the best accountant you can find and a lawyer with whom you're comfortable. You read above about some of the complexities of setting up a corporation, getting the right licenses, and other business matters, and you're just in the early stages of running your own business! As you get down the road, your financial situation will become more involved, and chances are that from time to time you'll need to consult on legal matters.

You might not think these professionals are necessary to your business now, but they will be. Even if you're confident that you can manage your business's financial books on your own, it's not likely that you're a skilled financial manager who can guide your business through the tangles of debt and investment that may lie ahead. Let's have a brief look at how professional help can benefit your business, and how you can go about finding the right people to steer you and your business into the future.

If for no other reason, you should have an accountant to handle your business tax work. Between federal, state, and local taxes, you'll need someone who keeps up with the codes of each authority, and who can make sure you pay the taxes you are supposed to pay—and not a penny more. It's not a crime to pay as little tax as the law allows, but it is a crime to avoid paying taxes that you are obligated to pay.

Most accountants can provide bookkeeping services, but it's usually better to manage part of this work yourself; there are plenty of excellent computer-based bookkeeping systems available, allowing you to save quite a bit of money. Before you buy a computer-based program, however, locate an accountant and find out which of the many systems available he or she works with and which would be best for you to use. Some accountants will even give you the program you need in order to plug you into their system quickly and efficiently.

In addition to handling the tedious chores related to the preparation of tax forms, accountants can be worth their weight in gold when it comes to tax planning. No one is in a better position than an accountant to help you minimize your anticipated tax obligations. A good accountant also should be able to help with projecting revenue streams and overall economic performance, as well as to prevent you from getting into financing arrangements that may be inappropriate for a home-based business. And, when you are ready to sell your business and spend the rest of your time at the beach, an accountant can be the one who prevents you from selling too low, or pricing so high that no one makes an offer. You'll read more about finding the right accountant in chapter 8: Managing Your Business Finances.

Hopefully, it will be a rare occasion that you need a lawyer. In the event that you do, however, it's a lot better to have an established contact than to be forced to find a lawyer in the Yellow Pages at the last minute, after you've been handed a summons to appear in court. Here are just a few of the situations you might encounter where legal assistance is needed:

- Whenever you sign an agreement that involves a significant amount of money

- Whenever you sign an agreement that commits you to a long and time-consuming project or a very substantial sale
- Whenever you sign an agreement that is difficult to understand
- When you agree to take on an employee who might become your competitor at some point in the future
- When you have intellectual property that you need to protect
- Whenever you alter the form of your business or start another business

These are just a few of the more common situations which usually require the professional assistance of an attorney. Selecting the right lawyer assures that he or she will be able to respond quickly and professionally in the event that you require assistance.

Choosing the Right Candidates

When seeking both an accountant and a lawyer, start by asking for recommendations from people you know who are in similar businesses. Make sure that the accountants and lawyers you consider have experience that relates to your business and are capable of and interested in working with start-up firms.

Accountant Performance Rating Tips . . .

Apart from the basic qualifications, think about these factors after you have started to work with your accountant:

- Has your accountant been available when needed?
- Have reports been submitted to you on a timely basis?
- Are all charges, other than the regular charges, itemized and clearly documented?
- Has the accountant been helpful in explaining reports you do not understand?
- Has the accountant involved you in all decisions other than those which you both agree do not require consultation?
- Has the accountant informed you of tax and legislative changes that could impact your business?

Some accounting firms will charge by the project, some by the hour, and some use either a retainer or some form of service package. As you might imagine, if you bought an accountant's services on some sort of cafeteria arrangement, you would probably end up paying more than you might if you engaged the accountant to provide a package of services you will need regularly.

The larger the accounting firm, the less likely you will be to have any regular access to the top people in the firm. The smaller the firm, the better the access, but you will be limited to a smaller body of overall experience.

The question of whether or not your accountant should be a Certified Public Accountant (CPA) or just an accountant is an important one. Anyone can be called an accountant, but in order to be a CPA, a person must have extensive educational credentials and then must pass very rigid tests. In order to maintain CPA status, individuals must continue to study the changing laws and meet the standards for state licensing after regular examinations.

Once you have identified several accountants who seem to be appropriate for the business you are planning, the best way to make the choice is to interview each one. If you have already done your business plan, be sure that each candidate has had an opportunity to review it. If you haven't done the plan yet and are waiting until you have an accountant to help you, be prepared with all the data you have at hand. It will be even more helpful to provide the prospective accountants with this material in advance of your meeting. Give them time to get a feel for what you are doing now and what you plan to do in the future.

Ask the individuals you meet with for their credentials as they relate to your type of business. If there are others in the accounting firm, ask about whomever else may also work on your account. Ask about specialties, and who will be the point person on your account—your contact. You should also ask about any support staff, such as bookkeepers, with whom you might interact if you give the firm your business.

Once you are comfortable with the answers to your questions about staff and professional skills, the question of charges is next. It's likely that you will either be offered a package deal, or a cafeteria type of usage of the firm's services. If you are relatively knowledgeable about accounting and finance, the cafeteria approach probably makes the most sense. But, if you are like most other start-up business owners, you will probably be better off signing on to a package program that will include all of your financial management needs. These programs lump the services of individuals in the accounting firm into one regular fee. If you go the cafeteria route, ask about how the firm differentiates its rates. You don't want to pay the same hourly rate for the firm's bookkeeping services as you do for the firm's chief tax accountant. The more routine work you can do yourself, the lower the fee will be.

The best way to find an attorney who will be most able to help you is to seek referrals from others who are working in the same business as you. If you strike out, check the listings of any professional or trade associations you belong to. Many maintain listings as well as comments from members on how helpful the lawyer in question might have been in specific situations. If your local library has a copy of the Martindale-Hubbell Law Directory, that's also a good place to start (or you can check out www.martindale.com). The one thing you want to avoid is talking to your uncle's wife's third cousin who is a lawyer—unless, of course, he or she happens to specialize in your field.

Here Are Some General Guidelines to Help You in Your Search:

Ask if there is a charge for the first meeting, or initial consultation. Some lawyers will meet with you briefly to make sure neither of you would make a mistake by establishing a relationship. If you get to the point of an initial consultation, it's fair for the attorney to charge you for the time spent.

Ask the attorney for details about his or her experience handling work similar to the work you will need done. Most lawyers can tell you in general terms what they have done, and for whom, without revealing any confidential details. (If an attorney seems to be hedging on details, it's probably not because he has nothing to say, but because he may have too much to say that he cannot divulge.)

If it isn't already apparent, ask about the type of clients the attorney represents. If none are familiar, ask how his or her experience with these clients relates to the issues on which you might need counsel.

Try to see where you will stand in terms of the size and importance of the other clients the attorney works with. You want to make sure that even though you may be small relative to his or her other clients, that you will still get the service you need when you need it. If the lawyer you choose is recognized as a specialist in your field, all the better; however, remember that specialists can be costly.

Legal fees can be high, so make sure you know what fees will be involved. You may be charged by the hour, or the attorney may be willing to work for a percentage of any settlement in your favor. Make sure you and the attorney see eye to eye on the money before any counseling is begun. If others on the staff, such as researchers, are to be involved, ask how their services will be billed.

If you are working with a large firm, make sure that you meet with and approve of the staff attorney who will handle your case. Don't hesitate to ask if there might be another attorney to consider if you are uncomfortable with the person the firm might assign to your case.

Ask about the kind of backup the staff has. If research is involved, you need to know that those doing it understand the elements of your case.

Finding and getting to know qualified professionals who can guide your business is not only a good business move, it will be assuring and give you much needed confidence as you move ahead.

Frequently Asked Questions

1. *How do I know which business structure is right for me?*
   You'll need to get as much information as you can about the various types of business structures, compare the pros and cons, and decide which one seems best suited to your home-based business. Most entrepreneurs start out as sole proprietors or in partnerships, which are basically sole proprietorships run by two or more people. There may be some reason, however, that your business would be better structured as a corporation, and, if you're wondering about that, you should consult a good accountant or business lawyer. Remember that if you begin as a sole proprietorship, you can always incorporate down the road.

2. *Why do I need to pay for the professional services of a lawyer and accountant when I feel I can handle those areas myself?*
   The answer to your question is contained in your question and it is the word "professional." You might be the best and smartest businessperson around, but if you're not trained in both law and finances, it's a bad idea to try to handle complicated legal or financial issues on your own. John Sortino, the successful entrepreneur you met in chapter 1, is adamant about paying experts to do the work of experts. His advice is to do well what you know how to do well, and pay someone to do well what you can not.

03

Getting Started II: Practical Steps to Getting Your Business off the Ground

Once you've waded through the legalities of business structure, licenses and licensing, registering a name for your company, setting up banking accounts, and locating professional services, it's time to launch your business by figuring out who your first customers or clients will be, how you'll price your product or services, what your business logo will look like, and other practical matters. It's also time to take a look at your competitors to see what you can learn from them. So, roll up your sleeves and let's get down to business.

Setting Fees and Prices

How much to charge for a product or service is a question that's been pondered by nearly everyone who has ever started a business. You want to charge enough, of course, to make a profit and assure that your business will be successful. On the other hand, you don't want to charge more (or at least not much more) than your competitors and risk driving away business.

Products are a little easier to set pricing for than services, which are harder to get a handle on and which contain more variables. Be assured that there have been countless discussions regarding this issue among freelance writers, consultants, and others who offer services. You know that how much you charge for your product or services will affect many aspects of your business, but how do you know where to set your prices?

One thing you don't want to do is to set your prices or fees lower than anyone else's with the thought that customers will flock to you and you'll be overwhelmed with business and make tons of money. It's a mistake to cut your profit margin to the point where you have to work yourself to death just to sell enough to cover expenses and have a little bit left over. Charging less than anyone else does can actually impact your business negatively, as it could result in the perception that the product or services you offer are inferior.

If you're reselling a product and hoping to make a profit, you need to be certain, of course, of what you paid for it. This sounds obvious, but you'd be surprised at the number of business owners who order from different distributors and yet don't keep detailed records on how much they've paid for merchandise. So, be sure you know what you paid for each item you're going to sell. Once that's clear, you'll need to consider your expenses.

Let's say that you sell specialized gift baskets. If the basket and the items in the basket cost you $20, and you sell the baskets for $50, your markup is $30 for each basket. This sounds great, and you probably think you're going to make a fortune selling gift baskets. Until, that is, you start thinking about the real cost of the baskets to you. This is called the cost of goods sold, and it definitely affects your bottom line.

With everything produced, either products or services, there are costs associated with the production. You've got to buy the materials that you put into those gift baskets. If you have an employee or employees to help you, you've got to pay them. You've got to have the equipment you need to pack, process, and distribute the baskets. The more money it costs you to produce your product, the less profit you'll make on it, unless you can get away with selling it for an exorbitant price to a market that doesn't mind paying it.

The cost of goods sold includes raw materials, time and labor, supplies, purchases, overhead, packaging, shipping, change of inventory, and some miscellaneous expenses. Some of these costs are easier to control than others, and some vary more than others. Obviously, it's important to keep your costs as low as you can, in order to increase your profit. You don't, however, want to cut corners to the point that you jeopardize the quality of your product and make is unsaleable. That's a sure way to put yourself right out of the market. So, your markup on the baskets has to be enough to cover your expenses and leave some money left for profit.

Where your business is also can affect your pricing. You've probably had the experience of shopping or eating or paying for recreational activities in different locales and noticed how the pricing varies. The Reuben sandwich you order in a corner deli in Allentown, Pennsylvania, for instance, is likely to cost far less than one you'd order in a New York City deli. Generally, you'll pay higher lawyer fees in a metropolitan area than you would in a rural setting. You'll pay more for a hotel in Philadelphia than in Springfield, Illinois, and more for your child's day care in Boston than in the little town of Broadhead, Wisconsin.

Your customers also help to determine where you set your prices, whether for services or products. If you're dealing with an upscale clientele that doesn't balk at paying $75 for a haircut, go for it. If you're competing with the walk-in haircut place at the mall, however, you'd better rethink that.

When trying to set a price for services, it's really important to know your competition, and the range of prices being charged within your business area. You can get an idea of this by perusing advertising and checking out competitors' Web site. If you work project by project, such as a graphic designer, or writer, or consultant, or event planner does, you'll need to think about whether to charge an hourly fee or a project fee.

There's plenty of precedent for charging by the hour, and many clients prefer it to a project fee. One of the major benefits of charging by the hour for you is that you will be able to charge for hours that you never anticipated when you first discussed the engagement with the client. Most clients will ask you to give them an estimate of the time you expect to spend on the project so they will have an idea of what the fee will be. This isn't unreasonable, and when you do give them the estimate, you should include a list of all the tasks you see as necessary in order to complete the assignment. However, you should also explain that anything that keeps the clock running past the estimated time will be itemized and billed.

If you charge a per project fee, your internal standard still should be based on your hourly rate. You'd have to make your best guess on the time needed to complete the job, but also consider what contingencies might pop up that were never considered when the assignment was first discussed. If you don't plug in a figure for unanticipated work, you will lose money. Once you gain enough experience in handling a particular type of project, you'll be able to better know how much to charge per project.

Contingency Agreements

If your business is one in which you provide some type of consulting or related service, you may run into a client who suggests payment based on whether or not your advice pans out. This is not where you want to go for a number of reasons. First of all, you will probably have absolutely no control over the way the client implements the plans, suggestions, and ideas you propose. For that reason, you could provide the best advice on the planet, and have it turn out to have absolutely no benefit. Second, you will have no control over the environment in which the suggestions are used. And, third, unless you specifically offer to follow through with any implementation, you cannot guarantee your plan's success. After all, you are not operating in the client's business—you are serving as a consultant.

Some consultants agree to adjusted fees in return for a payment based on the success or failure of a plan. If you go that route, remember that any bonus money should always amount to more than you would earn if the client had agreed to your full fee, up front. You are taking a risk over which you have no control. I have no solid guidelines to offer for the amount a fee could be reduced in the event of failure, but you should at least be compensated for all of your out-of-pocket expenses, plus a slight reduction in your hourly fee.

What About Rate Variations for Different Clients?

It's not terribly unusual for those providing services to vary their fees with different clients. However, there must be a real reason for doing this, and you should be able to explain your reasons to clients, as you don't want to appear to be discriminatory. If you charge a first-time client a lower fee in order to encourage his business, just make sure that he fully understands that it is an introductory offer figure, and get his acknowledgment in writing if you can. If you bill at the lower rate for an agreed-upon period of time and then revert to your standard rate, and you can document this, you should be okay.

What Expenses Can You Charge to Clients?

It's common in some businesses to charge expenses to customers or clients. Lawyers tend to bill for everything, including postage and the money the telephone company charges them for individual calls. Engineering consultants usually bill for special computer time they must buy when working on some client assignments. Human resource consultants will usually bill the costs for testing materials they use in conjunction with corporate assignments. Graphic designers may charge for special paper or other supplies necessary to complete a project. Wedding planners keep careful track of expenses and create an accounting of them which the client is expected to pay. Whether you bill some expenses or not really needs to be determined by what is required by the project and what is already customary in your field.

Some professionals might charge for travel time, reasoning that time spent traveling to and from a client's office is time that could have been spent working on billable projects. Again, there is no one answer that fits all situations. If it's customary in your field to bill for travel time and other expenses, and your client expects that you will, then you should do it. You might consider setting a policy to bill for travel time and expenses if the travel period exceeds four hours, and if the travel is going to be frequent enough to eat into time that would not be available to do other work. Again, industry standards should be your guideline.

Expenses are always billed at cost, and supporting invoices and receipts should always accurately document your expense billing to a client. Just be sure that your client understands up front that you'll be including expenses in your billing.

Unfortunately, there's no magic formula for setting prices, and you may have to experiment a bit. By knowing your costs and understanding your market, you can develop a range of pricing in which you know for sure your price must fall.

Learning from the Competition

If you're willing to dig in, you can learn a lot more from your competitors than what they're charging for their products and services. You can experience what they're doing right and what they're doing wrong, check out who patronizes them and who doesn't, and look for new ideas you're your own business.

Some friends who own a small marketing, graphic design, and web design agency in Pennsylvania regularly scour the Web site of their competitors to find out who their clients are, new business they've received, and what messages they're putting out to clients and prospective clients. When one competitor shifted its focus from traditional project advertising to branding, a more comprehensive form of advertising, and its Web site was loaded with the names of new clients who had come on board, my friends decided they ought to look into branding, as well.

You can be your own best barometer when it comes to scouting out and learning from your competitors. Check out their ads or Web site and compare the businesses with one another. Which one would you most likely pay for its good or services? Why? If you're looking to start a landscaping business, check out the Yellow Page ads, all the Web sites of local landscapers, billboards, newspaper ads, and anything else you see. Which companies come off as being professional and impressive? Which ones don't? Why? What do their trucks look like? What kinds of business logos do they have? Where do you see their workers when you drive around town? Where don't you see their workers? What do the workers wear to work?

Put your family members and friends on alert and get them to help you scope out your competition. Once your business is underway, ask your customers about your competitors—what do they like about them? What don't they like? Don't come off as if you're snooping, just ask in an interested manner. This not only provides you with valuable information, it can move your customer relationships to a new level.

There are very few businesses in which you won't have competitors. Figure out a way to set your business apart from theirs, and learn what you can from them. Smart entrepreneurs never stop learning, and they know that their competitors can actually be friends in disguise.

Getting the First Client or Two

Once you've done your homework and jumped through the hoops and are ready to open your business, you'll need to attract some customers. Hopefully, you've gotten the word out about your business (you'll read more about that in chapter 11: Marketing Your Company) and people will be flocking to buy your products or services. On the other hand, you could experience a little lag time until the word about your business spreads, and you could find yourself becoming frustrated and discouraged.

So, how are you going to attract those first clients or customers to get your business underway? Consider the following suggestions.

Harness the power of e-mail. The Obama campaign took to the Internet during the 2008 campaign and reached millions of voters who contributed campaign funds and volunteer hours, greatly contributing to our President's victory in November. E-mail everyone you know that your business is open, and ask them to pass on the e-mail to everyone in their address books. Many people regularly e-mail one another about a good (or bad) restaurant they've visited, a new thrift shop they've discovered, or the great haircut they got at the new salon in town. E-mail is a proven tool; it's easy to do, and costs virtually nothing.

Be a walking advertisement of your services. You're all set to go with your pet care business except that you have no pets to care for. You might just have to borrow some dogs and start walking. Offer to walk your three or four of your neighbors' dogs (at the same time) and take them to the part of town where the most people will see you. Be sure you have a pocketful of business cards, and don't be afraid to hand them out. You'll be a true walking advertisement of your services, and let people know you're available.

Think about who you know. Identify those who might be looking for your product or service. If your business is child care, who do you know who has children? Or grandchildren? Or nieces and nephews? Circumstances change, and even those who have reliable child care at the moment could find themselves looking next week or month. Contact everyone you know who might need what you're selling, either immediately, or in the future.

Get into the business network. Join your local chamber of commerce or other business or civic group. Organizations such as Rotary, Junior Achievement, or the chamber of commerce offer great opportunities for you to meet other business people and spread the word about your venture. If you're young, see if there's a young businesspersons group in your area. The more contacts you acquire, the faster the word about your business will spread. Friends of friends, people you may never have met, probably know some of the people you should get to know. Put out the word, ask everyone, do whatever it takes to identify the names of real people as your key prospective clients. Remember that you only need a few good contacts to get started, and once started, the referrals are easy to get. In addition to networking, use whatever media is appropriate to make an impression on potential clients. I'm not talking about extensive advertising, but think about writing articles for the publications that your prospects read.

Try not to get discouraged. Waiting for your business to take off can be discouraging, but try to remain optimistic. Sometimes, all it takes is one or two clients or sales or projects to start things rolling, after which you'll be wishing you had a little more free time! Use the slow time to fine tune what you've already put into place, be aggressive with your marketing, and try to be patient. If you've established realistic goals, you may find that you're right on track, even though you feel you should be further along.

Generating a Great Business Logo

You want your business to stand out, and a great logo will help you to achieve that. Your business logo should be part of your overall marketing plan, but you'll want to have it as you're starting up to help you get recognized and to begin establishing a business, or corporate image within the marketplace. You want your logo to be eye catching, to stand out, and to be easily recognizable. Let's think of those business logos that are instantly recognizable, some of them so much so that they've become almost iconic.

Chiquita bananas	KFC
Coca Cola	Kodak
CitiBank	Legos
Dove Soap	McDonalds
FedEx	MTV
Ford	Nike
Fruit of the Loom	Pepsi
Good Year	Red Bull
Google	Shell Oil
Harley Davidson	Starbucks
Hummer	Texaco
IBM	UPS
Jeep	

You probably can picture most of these in your head, because you instantly connect the logo with the business name. That's market presence!

There are three basic types of business logos: font-based, which basically is just type that's been styled to make it unique, such as the IBM logo; those that illustrate what the business does, such as a music teacher incorporating musical notes in his logo; and abstract, such as the Nike swoosh.

While the Nike logo is surely one of the most famous logos, remember that the company has spent millions of dollars over a period of years to promote it and establish its brand identity. For our purposes, a logo that is descriptive of your business, or one that creates an immediate feeling of trust or warmth, is probably a better way to go than an abstract logo.

To help you get an idea of what you want your logo to look like, write a one sentence mission statement about your company, and then think of how you might depict that mission statement in a logo. Keep these tips in mind.

- Check out the logos of your competitors. Are they serious looking or fun? Your logo probably shouldn't convey a completely different image, but think about how you can make it a little different so it stands out.
- Keep it simple. An overly complicated logo may not be easy to reproduce, and you want your logo to work on everything, from your business cards to a billboard. Strive for a logo that works well both in color and black and white, and make it not more than three colors. Five color might look great, but it's expensive to reproduce, and three color can work just as well.

- If using a font-based logo, choose a font that matches your business image. A business consultant, for instance, would not use the same font as a party planner. One must convey authority, and the other, fun.
- Stay away from trendy. You want your logo to last, not to change seasonally along with fashion trends.

If you're not particularly creative or artistic, you might want to hire someone to help you create a logo. Yes, there are lots of online sites that offer free business logos, or templates you can buy to create your own, and, that might be okay for some businesses. Your logo, however, is very important in conveying who, and what your business is and does, and should be carefully considered.

You could approach an advertising agency to help you with your logo, but agency prices can be, well, pricey. Get online or ask around to see if someone knows a good freelance graphic designer. There are tons of designers who always are looking for extra work. Whatever you do, don't settle for a business logo you're not entirely happy with. That's like buying a pair of shoes that don't quite fit—you'll never be entirely comfortable.

Once you've got a logo that you like, use it in all your marketing efforts. It can't benefit your company if your customers and prospective customers don't see it.

Getting Your Business on the Web

Should your business have a Web page? Let's see. Where's the first place you look when you want to find a restaurant that serves Sunday brunch, or a veterinarian with 24-hour call service, or a full-service florist? If you're like a lot of people, you probably jump online and Google "Sunday brunch Philadelphia." The answer to the first question in this section is "yes, your business should have a Web site."

Your Web site doesn't need to be elaborate, or contain flash, or have sound, but a Web presence is nearly a necessity for a business, especially a home-based business that lacks the visibility of a storefront. A home-based business, for that matter, probably needs to rely on a Web site at least as much, if not more, than a retail business. A Web site will benefit your business in several ways. It will:

- Provide information about your business
- Help you to sell products or services
- Create a convenient manner for customers and potential customers to contact you

- Provide you with additional market presence

Before you hire someone to build your Web site, or, alternately, start building it yourself, take some time to think about what you want it to do. Do you hope to actually conduct business there? Or will it serve more as a marketing tool or a customer service enhancement? Can you make it easy for customers and others to find your site? How will you design the site so it's easy to navigate? If you've ever been on a Web site that's overly complicated and cumbersome to use, you know what a turn-off it is.

After you've given these questions some thought, get on line and cruise the web for a while. Especially take some time to check out the sites of other businesses in your industry and see what your competitors are doing.

If you've had experience setting up Web site, you may be able to build your own. Some business owners prefer this because it gives them complete control over the look and feel of the site. Remember, though, that your site needs to be as professional looking as your business cards, stationary, and other marketing materials. If you don't have a working knowledge of basic Web design, it's best to get some help.

If you can't afford to hire a professional to build your site, there are templates available on sites such as SiteDeluxe or Templatemonster. Some online templates are free, while others will cost a little bit to use.

If you decide to hire a professional to build your site, make sure you effectively communicate your expectations as to how you want it to look and what you want it to do. You'll need to meet with the designer, and don't let him or her rush you. It's your site, and the designer's job to build it to your wishes and expectations.

You'll need a domain name, or URL, for your site so that people can find you. You register your domain name through a service called a domain registrar. The cost of registering your name can be as little as a few dollars a year, or as much as thousands

A Word of Caution

If you know little about computers and nothing about Web design, think carefully before deciding to build your own site. An amateurish looking site will not impress potential customers, and could negatively impact your business.

of dollars a year if someone already controls the name that you've just got to have. Your domain name should be short and simple, perhaps simply the name of your business. If that's already taken, you could try combing the name of your business and the city in which you're located, such as www.sweetendingsminneapolis.com.

Your Web site will require a Web hosting service, which often can be obtained from your Internet access provider. This is a simple process if your Web site is uncomplicated, but hosting becomes more complex as your site does. You also can buy certain equipment that allows you to host your Web site at your location.

As we near the end of the first decade of the 21st century, it's practically unheard of for a business to not have an Internet presence. If you're intimidated at the thought of Web design, find some help, but don't avoid the task and miss out on the advantages of being online.

Frequently Asked Questions

1. *I'm all ready to get my resume consulting business going, but it seems like I can't find anyone interested in hiring me. Does this mean my business is going to fail?*
    Not at all. Finding those first clients can take some time, so you've got to patient. Continue to fine tune your marketing plan, talk to everyone you know, and ask others to spread the word. Once you do get a job, provide the best possible quality of work and service, and word of your business will begin to spread.

2. *I want to sell the gift baskets I make online. How do I get started?*
   You'll need to have a Web site, of course, with a registered domain name and site host. And, you'll need to invest in some e-commerce software and decide how you want to exhibit your baskets on the site so that customers can see what they look like. You also can use a service such as eBay or Yahoo Shopping as a turnkey solution for building an online store. Once your site is established, be prepared to monitor it carefully in order to provide good customer service and timely delivery of your product.

04 The All Essential Business Plan

Let's begin this very important chapter with two thoughts. The first is that, if you're planning on starting a business, or you've already taken steps on getting it started, you will need a business plan. The second thought is that the business plan must be your own, not one that you've found on the Web and "customized," or one that you "borrowed" from a friend who started her own business two years ago. Sure, you can look at all the plans you want, and you can gain valuable insights from reading actual business plans of established businesses within your industry. In the end, however, it's got to be your work.

Your business plan needs to be your own because it's your business. Your business plan is not only a collection of facts and financial information, it holds your dreams, your plans, and your aspirations. You might be able to learn from someone else's marketing plan, but her dreams and aspirations will never exactly match yours.

The Purpose of a Business Plan

Your business plan serves two primary purposes. It will be your roadmap as to where your business is and where it's going, and it will be a valuable marketing tool in the event that you are looking for investors or partners. In both of those events, it's important that your business plan is written as honestly and forthrightly as possible. Make sure that your goals are realistic, and don't downplay the challenges you anticipate because you think it could scare off potential investors.

A business plan is important regardless of the type of business you're starting. It will define your business, list your goals, and describe what you bring to the table. If done properly, it will help you to allocate the resources you already have and provide a plan for the acquisition of the resources that you must acquire. It should be able to help you predict where and what the rough spots might be, and how you should go about overcoming them. And it should point the way to systems you can use to manage progress.

A carefully conceived business plan should have milestones to help you determine whether or not you are on the right track. And probably most important, a good business plan should provide alternatives for course corrections as you sail along. No matter how carefully you plan, it will always be necessary to make changes. Some of those changes will involve major shifts in direction, while others will involve ways to advance those things you are doing right. Your plan should not be a straitjacket, but it should be rigid enough to keep you on track and flexible enough to allow you to drop things that aren't working and switch to better alternatives.

You can find lots of information—entire books—dedicated to the task of writing a business plan. Gathering too much information and advice can make what may already seem like a challenging task appear to be overwhelming. There are a lot of good resources available, with some of them listed in appendix II of this book, but many entrepreneurs rely on the Small Business Administration, which offers both a great business plan primer on its Web site, and teams of retired executives who can help you—for free! If you don't already know about SCORE (Service Corps of Retired Executives), get on the phone to your local SBA office and ask to set up an appointment. It's an amazing, valuable service available in many communities across the country. The SBA web site also provides an online business plan workshop, and a step-by-step guide for writing your plan.

What Information Should My Business Plan Include?

You can streamline the process of writing a business plan by spending some time thinking about the following questions, as recommended by the SBA:

- What service or product does your business provide, and what needs does it fill?
- Who are your potential customers and why will they buy a product or service from you?
- How will you let potential customers know about your business?
- Where will you get the money you need to start your business?

The answers to those questions will provide much of the information you need for your business plan. There are lots of different styles of business plans, and no specific manner or order in which they must be written. There are, however, necessary components that are common to every plan. Your business plan should include the following elements:

- Table of Contents
- Executive Summary
- Market and Industry Analysis
- Business Overview
- Marketing Plan
- The Competition
- Plan of Operations
- Management Team
- Funding Needs

Let's take a look at each of those categories and see what it entails.

Table of Contents

Don't sweat this section, it's just to give those reading the plan an idea of what's included. And, it will make a good impression because it shows that your plan is well organized.

Executive Summary

The executive summary, as the name implies, should summarize your business plan. Not to put any pressure on you, but sometimes this is the only part of a plan a potential investor will read. If it comes off as unprofessional or inadequate, the would-be investor might quit right there.

The executive summary should be only one to two pages long, so explanations of each section must be brief. You'll briefly include the products or services your business will provide, what sets your business apart, your target audience, the competition, marketing plan, objectives, and financial projections. The information should be optimistic, but not pie in the sky. You should state your plans for the future, any major obstacles you might encounter, and how you would circumvent those obstacles.

Market and Industry Analysis

This section defines who your potential customers are, and why they're going to buy your product or service instead of those of another business. Here is where you have an opportunity to point out what's really special about your business, and to support your belief that there's a good market for it. You'll need to capture the characteristics of your market that will contribute to the success of your business venture. If you're opening an at-home after school care center, for instance, you'd want to be able to prove there are enough two-parent-working families in your area to support it. To do that, you'd use census reports and other information to learn about your community. You could look at school trends. If two new elementary schools are under construction within your school district, that's a good sign of a growing population of young children.

Once you've identified your market, you've got to present your business in the context of the larger industry of which you belong. The Bureau of Labor Statistics (www.bls.gov) can provide valuable information, and there are some state and national child care provider organizations that may be useful. You'd want to present where the industry stands, and projections for its future. You can use charts or graphs to help get your points across. If your industry is a boom industry, which the child care industry is, according to the Bureau of Labor Statistics, you're on the right track. If you learn that the industry in which your business falls is predicted to be in decline, you might have a hard time convincing potential investors that your business is a great idea.

Business Plan Tip

It's especially important to have a clear picture of your business area, both in terms of the services needed now and in the future, and in terms of the competition you will face when you open your doors. You should have a clear vision of how you will address the economic trends that exist in the field now, and in the future. For example, as the current economy shrinks, some areas of your business may shrink, while others may grow. Any numbers you can plug into this thinking will be very helpful, as will be any ideas you have about shifting your business emphasis when the economic climate changes yet again.

Business Overview

Your business overview should be a comprehensive look at your business plans, all in the space of a couple of pages. The overview will start off with an explanation of the goals of the business. Get specific here. Where do you expect to be in a year? Five years? Do you plan to remain small, or are you planning to build a larger organization? What do you see for yourself in terms of personal self-improvement that might be required to start and build the business? This could include formal schooling, distance learning, or simply identifying your weak areas so that you can strengthen them by your day-to-day work experiences.

Explain what your legal structure will be. Will you start off as a sole proprietorship with plans to incorporate in five years? If you're going to have one or more partners, you'll need to provide insights of your partner relationships and the various roles you expect each partner to fill within the business. Be sure to outline the strengths of each person and illustrate how those strengths combine to assure all aspects of the business are covered.

List the products or services that you'll be providing, explain that the business will be run out of your home, and your anticipated opening date. You'll need to outline the resources that will be necessary in order to run your business; for instance, will you need to purchase a van with which to make deliveries, or a professional-quality oven in which to bake wedding cakes?

You also should include what type of record keeping system you plan to use and how the business will operate. If you have any initial investors, that information should be included in this part of your plan, as well.

Turn On the Spell Check

A business plan that is poorly written or contains misspellings and typos will not impress potential investors in your business. If you're one of those people for whom writing is difficult, be sure to ask somebody to proofread your business plan before you start passing it around. Or, there are writers who specialize in writing business plans who could assist you. Don't be afraid to ask for help. Your business plan is an important tool and should be prepared as professionally as possible.

Marketing Plan

You've described your market and how you fit within it, now you've got to tell how you're going to break into it. This part of your business plan needs to outline how you'll get the word out about your business, and how you intend to sell and track the sales of your product or services. You'll want to describe your pricing, and tell how you decided what to charge. This section will tell how you plan to promote your business, any networking opportunities you have, and share your ideas for special promotional events such as contests or giveaways.

You'll also need to describe your plans in terms of advertising, public relations campaigns, and other marketing opportunities. You should be familiar with the effectiveness of various media outlets in your area, and beyond your area, if applicable. For instance, would you do best to advertise on your local radio station, or is your target audience more likely to see an ad on the cable TV channel? A newspaper ad might be effective if your target market is an older audience, who tend to still read newspapers. Younger customers, as you probably know, are less likely to subscribe to the local paper. Be sure to include how much money you plan to spend on advertising, and be able to justify the expenditure by providing information such as "by advertising during drive time on WQRW's morning show, I will reach an average of 45,000 listeners each day." It's important to show that your marketing plan has been well planned and thought through. You'll learn much more about putting together a good marketing plan in Chapter 11.

The Competition

It would be nice if your business was the only one of its kind around, but chances are that you're going to have some competition. And, that's okay as far as your business plan goes. In fact, acknowledging your competition proves that there is, indeed, a demand for your product or service.

You'll want to get to know all that you can about your competitors so you can outline in your business plan how their businesses operate, where their locations are in comparison to yours, what share of the market they hold, and anything else that is pertinent. You need to know the strengths and weaknesses of your competitors so you can relate how your business will compare and how your product or services will be superior to theirs.

Don't be tempted to put your competitors down, or present them as inconsequential. You're merely trying to separate your business from those of your competitors and relate how you plan to set your goods and services apart from those that are currently available.

Plan of Operations

This part of your business plan will vary, depending on the type of business you're starting. The operating plan describes what is necessary to the operation of your business. This could include machinery or other equipment or stock. It could include information about suppliers, how you'll keep track of inventory, and, if you're manufacturing a product, a description of the manufacturing process. You'd also want to mention the delivery process of your product or service, if applicable

If you're a member of any industry organizations you should list them here, or mention those that you plan to join. Mention any licensing agreements you've made, steps you've taken to get variances, if necessary, and quality control measures you've put into place or plan to put into place,

It's unlikely that your at-home business will involve much manufacturing, but, if so, you'll have to explain where you'll get the materials you need, the facility in which the manufacturing will occur, and so forth. This section of your business plan will be much shorter for those starting service-based businesses who don't use machinery to produce goods. You may, however, want to include an outline of what you anticipate to be your daily business routine.

Management Team

Assuming that your home-based business will be starting out small, it's likely that your management team will include only one or two or three people – you, and perhaps a partner or two. This section of your plan will list the key players and tell why each one is qualified to lead the business and describe the roles that each will play.

Describing your management team is especially important if you're seeking start-up capital, as lenders want to know who would be getting their money. You'll need to include a short biography for yourself and other members of your team, outlining career history, educational background, professional affiliations, and so forth. Don't try to make these cute, and don't include any information that isn't relevant to the business.

Outline the primary responsibilities of each person, what their titles will be, and why each is qualified for the job. If you have a board of directors or business advisors, you should list them here and include a bit of background information on each. You also should include the names and contact information of your attorney, accountant, banker, insurance agent(s), and others who might play some role in your business.

Funding Needs

This section is pretty much the crux of your business plan, especially if you're seeking investors or might be looking for investors down the road. You've laid out the overview of what your business is, who your customers will be, how you plan to operate, and presented a lot of other information. This section is the place to reveal how you plan to finance your business, and that is a crucial piece of information.

You need to outline how much money you have available, how much more you need, and how long you anticipate it will take for your business to be at the point where any loans can be repaid.

Clearly state your financial needs, and tell how the money you have and obtain will be used. Will most of it go toward marketing? A fancy Web site to facilitate Internet sales? You'll need to be able to explain the justification for your expenditures, beginning with start-up costs and continuing with the longer-term costs of doing business.

Business Plan Tip

Unless you're particularly financially savvy or have written business plans in the past, it's probably a good idea to get professional help with this part of your plan. Ask your accountant or another qualified financial person to help you, but make sure you understand all the information presented in this part of your plan. You don't want to be caught off guard if prospective investors ask you questions about your finances.

Once you've stated how much money you'll need, describe how your company will generate profits. You'll need to include an income statement, balance sheet, and cash flow analysis for the first three to five years of your business, outlining how you plan to build the business and make it financially successful. You don't want to paint a gloomy picture here, but you don't want to be overly optimistic, either. Try to get a realistic overview of what you need and how quickly you'll be able to repay it, and present it in an understandable manner.

Other Items You Can Include in Your Business Plan

Depending on the particulars of your business, you might decide to include some extras with your business plan. These might include the following:

- A complete list of all the equipment you already have and that which you plan to buy, including any supplies that this equipment might require on a regular basis
- Studies, special reports, and relevant articles that relate to your business
- Any agreements, leases, and contracts that relate to your business and its home office location
- Lists of prospects, letters of endorsement, certificates, awards, and licenses needed to operate your business
- Magazine and journal articles relevant to your start-up

Once your business plan is written, don't be tempted to set it aside. You should consult it often, as it will serve to motive you and keep your business on track. If you see that you're lagging in some of your goals, figure out what you can do to advance them. Don't however, let your business become a slave to the business plan. It's intended to serve as a guide, but never to restrict the growth of the business. You might find your business going off in a direction that you never anticipated and is not mentioned anywhere in your business plan. As long as you continue moving ahead, you'll make your business a success.

Frequently Asked Questions

1. *Can I skip the business plan? I don't need investor capital, and my home office is ready to go.*
   You still should develop a business plan, even if its relatively simple. Just provide the information that's needed. Even though you may think everything is in place and have all the answers, it's a good idea to put together a plan to keep you on track as you move ahead.

2. *It seems like it could take a lot of time to create a successful business plan. How long should it take?*

    If you have all the information at your fingertips and in your files, it should only take a few days. However, the writing of the plan is the easy part. The difficult part is asking the right questions and then gathering the information you need to answer these questions. To do it right, you should assume that it will take at least two or three weeks. You may be in a position to work on your plan full-time, but if you will be doing it in your spare time, I'd suggest that you do it by gathering all the information you need first and then answering the questions before you start writing.

The majority of home-based businesses relies on clients to request and pay for their services. This applies to a wide variety of businesses, from house cleaning to professional consulting services. And, when you're just getting your business off the ground, or if business is slow at the time, it's tempting to agree to work with any client who comes along. Because of that tendency, there are all sorts of client horror stories floating around.

Cindy, an accomplished freelance writer was between jobs when she got a call from two doctors in a neighboring state who were looking for someone to write a book about a supposed huge new breakthrough they'd made in the field of sleep apnea. Their revolutionary discovery was going to not only cure sleep apnea, but could also prevent it from occurring, the doctors said. My friend, a seasoned medical writer, had some misgivings about the project, but her husband had recently lost his job and their daughter was finishing her junior year of high school and looking ahead to college. So, without properly screening the potential clients, she decided to pursue the project.

The doctors, who had gotten Cindy's name from another writer, were desperate for something to write their book, even though they had no publisher in place. They assumed that, once the book was written, publishers would be lining up to buy it. My friend explained to them that this generally isn't how the process works, but they insisted that she write the book—quickly. Because she needed the money, she signed an agreement, even though she knew in her gut it was a bad decision.

While she knew it was a bad decision to work with these guys, she couldn't fully anticipate just how awful it would be. The doctors insisted that she meet with them in person, meaning she spent hours and hours driving back and forth to their offices; they told her that she had sleep apnea and gave her a mask to wear while she slept; they nickeled and dimed every invoice she submitted; and they hounded her regularly to finish the project in an unbelievably short time. To make matters worse, there began to be friction between the two men, with Cindy feeling like she was stuck in the middle of their frequent disagreements over how the project should proceed.

Because she'd signed an agreement and had little choice, Cindy held up to her end of the bargain and finished the project. She finally was paid the agreed upon fee, but not without having to contact the doctors repeatedly until they paid her. She said it was probably the worst project she'd ever had, and the pay was nowhere near worth the hassle and unpleasantness of the experience.

Cindy's problem, of course, was that she was so anxious to get a project that she didn't properly screen the clients. Had she done so, she would have discovered before she signed the agreement to work for them that they were demanding, unreasonable, and actually very strange.

So, how do you go about screening clients, and how do you know which ones to work with, and which to decline? Let's take a look.

Work It Out in Advance

You'll be less likely to end up with a problem client (or project) if you've thought in advance about who you want to work for and the types of jobs or projects that you enjoy. While it's very tempting at first to want to take whatever work comes along, remember that agreeing to do a job that you can't do well, or that you're going to end up hating every minute of, isn't a good way to build your business. Clients won't be happy with work that isn't top notch, and you'll soon get burned out from working on jobs you don't enjoy.

When a potential client approaches you about a job or project, ask yourself the following questions:

- Is this a project I'm going to enjoy?
- Is this a project I'm going to be able to successfully complete?
- Is this a client with whom I'm going to enjoy working?
- Is there anything about this client that makes me uncomfortable?
- Is there anything about this project that makes me uncomfortable?
- Is the time frame set for the project a reasonable one?
- Is this fee I'll earn for this project reasonable for the amount and type of work it involves?

- Will this project perhaps lead to other jobs and help me to advance my business?

Now, of course, to be able to answer these questions, you've got to know a fair amount about the project and the prospective client. It doesn't matter what type of business you have, you need to gather information before you can decide whether or not to agree to work for someone. In most businesses, every job is different, and you have to be prepared to be flexible when gathering information. Some information you need, however, is common to every job.

Questions for prospective clients:

- What exactly do you expect that this project will entail?
- What's the time frame for the project?
- Are you offering me a set fee for this project, or will we work together to arrive at a price, either based on a project cost or an hourly fee?
- How did you find out about me?
- Have you worked with other business owners on similar projects?

Getting the client to discuss the project or job will allow you to get a feel for his or her temperament, as well as giving you the opportunity to learn more about the work.

It's important, however, that you voice your expectations and ideas concerning the project, as well as listening to what the client has to say, and make sure the client is receptive to what you say.

Avoiding Time Traps

Screening clients is very important, but, when you're starting out in your own business, time is money, so keep the screening process on track and as efficient as possible. One marketing consultant wrote in his blog that he uses a "speed dating" model when screening clients. He has a set list of questions he asks each one, and is able to determine within eight minutes which he wants to work with and which he doesn't.

The ability to build rapport with the people you work with is critical for success. You may have the best ideas in the world, but if you cannot connect with the people who want and need them, you will have difficulty being successful in your own business. It is critically important to always be sensitive to the needs and interests of your clients. You need to know a lot more about each person than just the details of the project you've been engaged to work on. Early on you should be able to detect which individuals you interact with are supportive of your ideas, and which individuals are not.

Once you and a prospective client have exchanged ideas and you've gathered the information you need, you'll be in a good position to decide whether or not this particular client and job are right for you. And remember, this will get easier over time. The more clients and experience you have in whatever field you're working, the better you'll be able to differentiate which clients and projects are right for you.

Screening Clients by Telephone

Most initial screenings of clients probably will take place over the phone. Even if a prospective client contacts you by e-mail, it's best to arrange for a phone call or personal meeting if you're going to discuss the prospect of working together.

The first thing you should ask is how the person heard about your business. Don't forget to take notes while you're talking, as this sort of information will be valuable as you assess your marketing plan. If you've distributed a service guide or other source of information about your business, ask the prospective client if she received a copy of it. If not, you can offer to send one.

Begin by asking the client to describe the job on which you'll be working if you agree to work together. Listen not only to what she tells you about the job, but to her tone of voice and the attitude that she conveys.

If the project sounds like a good one and there's nothing about the phone conversation that lets you know the prospective client will be a problem, you can go ahead and schedule a meeting.

Screening Clients in Person

Regardless of whether the prospective clients comes to your office or you agree to meet her somewhere, be sure that you're prepared. Know what you want to ask and what information you hope to gain. If you're meeting somewhere other than your office, be sure you know exactly where you're going and take with you everything you might need—a laptop, notebook, calendar, your PDA, or whatever.

Keep your initial meeting professional and to the point, and don't drag it out to be longer than necessary. Be courteous and interested in the project and the client, but you don't need to learn about her family and what kind of car she drives during this meeting.

Unless there are special circumstances, don't commit to taking the job or project during this initial meeting. Even if the potential client is in a hurry to get the work underway, buy yourself a little time to think it over. You can simply say something like, "This certainly sounds like an interesting project, and I'm very glad to have met with you. I will give it some thought and call you first thing in the morning to discuss it with you further." That gives you some breathing room, while at the same time telling the prospective client that you're interested.

Sometimes You've Got to Just Say No

Sometimes you'll know right away that a job just isn't for you. A woman in Florida asks you to rework the manuscript she's written about her out of body experiences and the spiritual relationship she enjoys with a famous film actor (completely unbeknownst to him!) Just say "no." A guy from the next town wants you to take care of his three pit bulls while he goes off to the casinos for a week—the same three pit bulls about which you've heard horror stories from other pet sitters. Just say "no." A friend of a friend of a friend would like you to plan her daughter's 16th birthday party, and, by the way, since you know each other, would you consider giving her a substantial discount in exchange for recommendations if she likes your work? Just say "no."

Sometimes you'll find it necessary to turn down a client you'd love to work with because you've got too much work already on your plate, or it would be a rush job and you've got a family vacation scheduled, or you're helping to care for a sick family member and just can't figure out the life/work balance right now. In those events, it's best to be honest and to express your regret to the client. Tell her that, although you're unable to accept this particular project, you'd very much be interested in working together when your current situation changes. That leaves the door open for future work and possible client relationship.

Every entrepreneur has his or her own level of tolerance for clients and jobs, and some are more likely, for various reasons, to agree to work with someone who they sense will be difficult. You're the only one who can decide. If, however, at any time you feel threatened by a client, or that you're in an extremely uncomfortable or dangerous situation, remove yourself from the project completely as quickly as you can, and make it clear to the client that you have no interest in working with her again. If the situation is extremely serious, you may have to consider contacting the police or a lawyer to assist you.

Frequently Asked Questions

1. *I'm just getting started in my business and am very anxious to get my first clients. Shouldn't I take whatever comes along and be glad for it?*
   Not necessarily, for a couple of good reasons. One, you're just getting started, and the last thing you want is for your first few jobs to turn out to be disasters. That could be extremely encouraging and even lead you to question whether or not you've done the right thing by starting your own business. Two, agreeing to work with a client or take a job that you know isn't right for you will result in less-than-great work, which could reflect poorly on you in the future.

2. *How can I turn down a client without alienating him or her?*
   If you can't accept a project when asked, but would like to maintain a relationship with the prospective client, be honest about your situation. Explain why it is you can't agree to work with the client at this time, but make it clear that you'd certainly be interested in future opportunities. Offer to stay in touch with the client, and make sure that you do.

---

06 | Understanding and Serving Customers

Way back in chapter 1 you read that one of the advantages of having your own business is that you get to wear a lot of hats. In this chapter's discussion about customer service, we need to add another hat that business owners sometimes must wear. In addition to wearing the hats of a CEO, marketing professional, customer service representative, bill collector, sales director, business development manager, and custodian, some days it will benefit you to wear the hat of a psychologist.

People are complicated, and your customers (unless you're running a business geared toward pets, and even then you have to deal with the pets' owners) are people. You'll also need to wear the psychologist hat if you have employees or during any business dealings with others. It's particularly important, though, when dealing with your customers, who, of course, are vital to your business.

Customer service isn't rocket science, but some people seem to be much more intuitive about it than others. We've probably all been the objects of poor customer service, and it can be beyond frustrating.

Consider this scenario: You're running a little late on your way to pick up your son at day care when you remember that you promised to pick up your husband's dry cleaning today. It's much easier to perform that errand without your five-year-old, so you decide to stop by on your way to the day care center. You rush in and stand in front of the counter, only to have the two cashiers ignore you as they gossip about the state of Jon and Kate's marriage, or discuss some other banality. You immediately begin to feel irritated, in addition to already feeling pressured by your time situation. The cashiers continue to ignore you, so you start tapping the edge of your credit card on the counter—hard. When they continue to ignore you, you slam your keys down on the counter, which, at last, causes them to acknowledge you and ask if they can help you. By the time you gather your husband's dry cleaning, pay, and leave the store, you're upset and angry, and still in a hurry—which raises the possibility of an accident or some other misfortune. You also feel bad for expressing your irritation in an inappropriate manner by slamming your keys on the counter, and wish you would have handled things differently. By the time you pick up your son and get home, you've pretty much decided to find a new dry cleaning establishment.

That example of poor customer service is tame compared to some of the nightmares you read about, watch on YouTube, or hear about from others. A Washington, D.C. blogger had a video recorder running when a Comcast serviceman fell asleep on his couch during a service call. A New York blogger became famous a few years back when he recorded the last five minutes of a service call with an AOL representative, who told the blogger he was making a big mistake and then yelling at him as the blogger tried to cancel his AOL account. It's clear that there's no shortage of bad—really bad—customer service out there.

On the flip side, there are plenty of examples of rude customers, as well, who can make it very difficult for sales representatives to provide excellent service. Those incidents don't seem to be as widely discussed, though, and, as a business owner, you'll need to pay the most attention to the service you provide. And, in order to do that, you'll have to put on your psychologist hat and turn your attention to understanding what customers want and expect when dealing with a business.

Understanding What Customers Want

Of course, not every customer wants the same thing. A McDonalds customer is looking for something different than one dining at the pricey Ruth's Chris Steakhouse. A customer looking to purchase an engagement ring at Tiffany's has different expectations than someone shopping at Wal-Mart. Still, nearly every customer has some common expectations when purchasing a product or service. These include:

- **Acknowledgement.** A simple "thank you for your business" indicates to the customer that their visit has been acknowledged. Even if a customer doesn't buy anything, it's nice to acknowledge her presence.

- **Effort.** When you ask, "may I help you?" it indicates that you're willing to make an effort for your customer. Never act like you're doing a customer a favor by agreeing to help her.

■ **Willingness to solve a problem when one occurs.** Failure by a sales associate to acknowledge a problem is incredibly frustrating for customers. A friend, Lisa, had a terrible restaurant experience and sent an e-mail to the manager afterward, respectfully explaining what had happened during her visit and expressing why she was so dissatisfied. Not only did the manager not indicate any willingness to solve a problem, he, in rude language, advised Lisa not to return to the restaurant, as if the unpleasant experience had been her fault. Not one to take rudeness sitting down, Lisa forwarded the manager's e-mail to her entire mailing list and asked everyone to respond to the manager. Many of her loyal friends informed the manager that, not only would they never again visit the restaurant, they would advise everyone they knew to avoid it, as well.

■ **Understanding of her needs.** A customer who needs to explain what she's looking for four times, and perhaps to four different people, is not likely to be a satisfied customer. Company representatives should be well versed regarding all products and services, and quickly able to identify what a customer needs.

■ **Efficiency.** As with the situation in the dry cleaning shop described earlier, it's frustrating for a customer who is in a hurry—or even for one who is not—to witness the person who is waiting on him making no effort to act in an efficient manner. People have different speeds at which they operate, and some are naturally quicker than others. Customers, however, value at least an effort at being quick and efficient.

■ **Choices.** Burger King introduced its "Have it Your Way" slogan in 1974, enticing customers with the thought of custom-made burgers. Thirty years later, after spending millions of dollars on other, major ad campaigns, the restaurant chain returned to "Have it Your Way" because it most resonated with customers. We live in a country where customers have lots of choices and options about just about everything. Consider the choices you have when purchasing a cell phone or cell phone plan, or just go and look at the selection of toothpastes in your grocery store. Customers are used to choices and options, and expect them in nearly every circumstance.

■ **Consistency.** People like to know what to expect. It's why so many people eat breakfast at the same diner every morning or never stay at anything but a

Hampton Inn when they travel. There's something comfortable about knowing that the Big Mac you buy in New York City will be nearly identical to the one you buy in San Francisco or Chicago. Customers also like consistency and dependability when it comes to customer service.

- **Best value.** Not every customer is looking for the cheapest price around, but every customer wants to believe that he got a good value. A customer might be willing to pay more for a bracelet at a jewelry store at which a sales associate explains the features of the piece than she would at a discount store where it's simply displayed on a shelf. That's because the sales associate added value to the bracelet by talking about it to the customer. A grocery shopper might be willing to buy a name brand can of tomatoes instead of the store brand, even though the name brand cost 50 cents more, because she perceives that the name brand is a better value.

- **Confidentiality.** Gossiping or talking about one customer to another is a sure way to lose sales. What transpires between you and customer should remain private, unless there are special circumstances and you get the customer's permission to discuss it.

Positive Surprises

Excellent customer service providers will go out of their way to provide positive surprises for customers. Positive surprises are value-added features that often cost little or nothing, but perform wonders at generating good will and customer loyalty. A positive surprise can be as simple as a pretty paper bag instead of a plastic sack, or as stunning as an upgrade to first class on a plane trip. Consider the following examples of positive surprises, and the reactions they resulted in.

A husband reserving a room at a bed and breakfast in Charleston, South Carolina mentioned over the phone that their trip was in celebration of his wife's 50th birthday. When they arrived, their room was ready, complete with a 50th birthday card and a nice bottle of wine. The couple no doubt will stay at the same B&B on their next visit.

You leave work early to be sure you're at home when the serviceman arrives to fix your dishwasher. The expected arrival time comes and goes, but five minutes later the phone rings. The service guy tells you that he's across town and traffic is crawling because of an accident on the bypass. He expects it will be at least half an hour to 45 minutes before he can get to your place. You tell him not to worry, because, now that you know you've got a half hour window, you can run down to the grocery store and get what you need for dinner that night. While sitting and waiting for service would have been frustrating and resulted in wasted time, the simple courtesy of a phone call enable you to move ahead with your day and get started with dinner for your family. You're so impressed that you call the appliance store and tell the manager how much you appreciated the thoughtfulness of his technician.

A pet owner went to pick up her Golden Retriever at the kennel upon returning home from vacation and noticed that the dog had been bathed and brushed was sporting a green bow on his collar. The dog owner was initially annoyed, because, although her Golden looked very handsome, she hadn't requested any grooming services and was expecting that the cost for them would be added onto her bill. The kennel owner, however, explained to her that she'd had some extra time the previous day and, because the Golden was such a sweet dog, she decided to give him a bath. It had been her pleasure, she said. You thank her profusely, add a tip to your kennel bill, and schedule your dog for another stay during your upcoming business trip.

Customers love positive surprises, and they go a long way in promoting your business. Remember that it's very, very easy these days for anyone to spread the word, either in a positive and negative manner. While it seems to be human nature to complain more so than to spread good news and be appreciative, customers will tell others when they've been treated nicely or a salesperson has gone above and beyond the call of duty to create a positive experience.

The Personal Touch

An online seller of fashionable, and expensive, shoes writes a personal note to every customer who buys a pair of shoes from her site. She and her seven employees sometimes spend hours in a day writing as many as 200 notes, but her customers love them. Some customers even send back notes, thanking her for the one they received.

In many ways, we live in a very impersonal society. We can run through self-checkout at the grocery store, eliminating any contact with a cashier who might chat with you as she scans your groceries and packs your bags. You can get cash from the ATM, eliminating the need to interact with a bank teller. You can text or e-mail someone rather than talk to them. Many people prefer these impersonal means of conducting business because they think it saves time and is easier. However, and again, here is where you'll need to wear your psychologist hat, most people desire to have connections to other people, and to know that they're recognized and appreciated.

So, while the self-checkout at the grocery store might be convenient, it's still nice for someone to be at the door when you leave to thank you for shopping there today and ask if you need help in getting your groceries to the car. Greeting a customer with a handshake, or at least a friendly smile, goes a long way in setting a positive tone with which to conduct business.

If your business provides a service, you might consider following up with a postcard, thanking the customer for his business and urging him to feel free to call with any questions or concerns.

Face to Face or over the Phone

Providing excellent customer service is equally important whether you're dealing with a customer face-to-face or over the phone. Experiencing poor customer service while trying to conduct business over the phone can be incredibly frustrating, and it's really important, as a business owner, that you're aware of how customers are treated when they call your business.

Did you ever call and have someone pick up the phone sounding grumpy or irritable? How does that make you feel? Chances are that you end up feeling as grumpy and irritable and the person who answered the phone sounded. And, chances are that you're not going to be too anxious to conduct business with that person or they company she represents. Whether you answer your business phone or have employees who do, here are some tips you should keep in mind:

- If at all possible, have a person, not a machine, pick up your phone. Customers hate getting an electronic runaround when they call a business, and they may be inclined to hang up instead of waiting. If you need to use an answering system, invite the caller to leave a message and promise (if you can keep the promise) to get back to him by the end of the business day. If that's not possible, tell the caller honestly when you'll be able to return the call, and make sure that you do so.

- Answer the phone by the third ring. Customers start to wonder what's going on if a business phone rings more than this. An unanswered phone relates a message of inefficiency and inattentiveness—qualities you don't want attached to your business.

- Sound enthusiastic and pleasant when you answer the phone. The voice of the person who answers the phone often is the very first impression the caller gets of the company.

- Identify the company and give your name when you answer the phone. Don't ever leave a caller wondering if she's reached the right number. Always provide your company's name, your name, and ask how you can be of assistance when you pick up the phone.

- Don't put your caller on hold for long periods of time. If a caller has a problem or question and you need a little time before you can provide a solution or answer, politely tell the caller that you need to look into the matter and you'll be happy to call her back as soon as you've got an answer for her. Putting someone on hold while you run around trying to solve a problem gives the impression that you don't value the customer's time.

- Speak clearly and slowly enough that the customer can understand you and doesn't have to ask you to repeat yourself.

- If you use an answering machine, update your message, as necessary. It's annoying to have a machine promise that someone will get right back to you, when that someone actually is on vacation and won't be returning calls for the next ten days, or the business is closed down for a holiday.

- Instruct anyone who might be answering the phone as to the proper way to do so. You might want to keep a list of guidelines next to the phone, and encourage everyone to use them so that customers get pretty much the same response every time they call. Remember that customers value consistency.

Customer Service in an Internet Business

Internet businesses have taken off, to be sure, and, while customers love the convenience of shopping online, they often are frustrated by a lack of customer service from Internet-based businesses. Most online businesses claim to offer e-mail support to customers, but a recent survey by JupiterResearch (jupiterresearch.com) revealed that more than a third of companies surveyed took at least three days to respond to a customer, and many didn't bother to respond at all.

Clearly, it's easier to brush off a problem or complaint when you don't need to deal face-to-face with a customer, but to do so will alienate a customer equally as much. Internet businesses have become notorious for poor customer service, with many customers complaining that they can't even find a phone number to call if they have a problem. If you run an Internet-based business, check out a book by author Jim Sterne called "Customer Service on the Internet."

Using Technology to Improve Customer Service

While customer service and technology sometimes seem to be at odds with one another, there actually are software programs designed to facilitate good customer service. These programs are known as Customer-relationship management (CRM) software, and are designed to let users maintain records of customer interactions or send automated messages if service issues remain unresolved. While these programs are helpful to companies in which management wants to be able to track employees' contacts with customers, they probably aren't necessary in small firms with just one or two people handling customers.

Popular CRM programs for small businesses include NetSuite (netsuite.com), ACT! (act.com), Salesforce.com, RightNow (rightnow.com) and Microsoft Dynamics (Microsoft.com/dynamics). If you go the CRM route, experts recommend that you adapt the programs to your company, and use them in conjunction with personal customer service, not as a substitute for it.

Technology also can aid in your customer service efforts by allowing you to send follow up e-mails to customers or notices reminding them of upcoming events or specials.

Training Employees to Provide Excellent Customer Service

After you, your employees are the primary reflections of your company. It's very important to make sure they understand that everything they do within the company reflects on your business, especially the manner in which they relate to customers.

If customer service is important to you, you need to make it clear that it must be equally important to employees. Make sure that employees understand your expectations, and don't take for granted that they understand the basics of customer service. It would be a good idea to schedule a time for you to meet with employees and review the list of customer expectations printed earlier in this chapter. You might type up a phone script and have employees practice how they'll greet customers who call. Be sure they know to greet customers politely and to provide information in a pleasant manner. And, be sure that every employee understands the chain of information, so that if someone can't answer a question or provide the help that's needed, she can identify the person who can.

If you witness one of your employees providing outstanding customer service, be sure to acknowledge her actions and consider providing some sort of reward. Many companies provide bonuses or other incentive for employees who go above and beyond the call while serving customers.

Remember that you set the tone within your company for customer service, and you need to be a role model for your employees. Excellent customer service, however, needs to be a company-wide effort with everyone involved. Make it clear that a failure to do so will not be tolerated.

Dealing with an Unpleasant Customer

Customer service is vitally important to any businesses that deal with customers, but treating customers in a kind and respectful manner is not always easy. We've probably all encountered people who are nearly impossible to please, or those who are incredibly rude, angry, or inappropriate.

The times when you're forced to deal with these problems customers also require your psychologist's hat. You've got to know how to respond appropriately to someone who is angry or rude, and that requires some understanding of human behavior, as well as some advance planning.

A customer who is upset and taking his anger or frustration out on you desires several things from you.

- He wants to know that you're willing to help him. If a customer is angry because of a problem he's having with a product, or is dissatisfied with service he's received, he wants the matter to be addressed and the problem solved. Knowing that you're making an effort on his behalf will tend to placate him, even if you're not able to immediately solve the entire problem or remedy the situation.

- He wants you to acknowledge that he's upset or angry. Telling someone that you understand that he's upset validates his feelings, which often will help him begin to feel less angry. Being asked to tell you why he's upset also lets him know that you are concerned about him as a customer and interested in his problem.

- He wants to have some control over the situation. If a customer feels that he's being given a runaround or there's no solution to his problem, he experiences a lack of control, which can increase anger and frustration. Don't ever say, "I'm sorry, but there's nothing I can do about that," when addressing a problem with a customer. The truth is, it's up to you to figure out what you can do about it, and to try to give the customer some options as to how the matter can be handled. That gives him a sense of control over the situation, and, generally, his anger and frustration will lesson.

Difficult customers must be addressed, but never make the mistake of beginning or joining in an argument with them. Situations that begin small sometimes turn into major incidents, and that's something you want to avoid at all costs. If you see an employee becoming involved in an incident with a customer, separate the employee from the customer immediately and handle the situation with the customer yourself, dealing later with the employee. Remember that situations in which anger is present can escalate quickly, with potentially ugly, or even dangerous, results.

Recognize, and encourage your employees to recognize situations that have the potential to escalate, and to diffuse them by refusing to involve yourself. Don't let a customer "push your buttons" or goad you into arguing with him. If you feel yourself getting angry, say something like, "I'm very sorry, but I'm going to need to have you speak to someone else about this. Give me just a moment please to find the right person."

If you ever are in a situation in which you feel threatened by a customer, don't hesitate to ask for help. If there's no one around and you feel that you're in danger, ask the person to leave immediately. If he won't leave, call 911.

Our relationships with other people can be the most rewarding aspects of our lives, but also can be challenging, for the stakes are high. Cultivating good relationships with customers will benefit your business tremendously, and give you a huge advantage over businesses that are unable or unwilling to do so.

Frequently Asked Questions

1. *How can I know how my customers wish to be treated when they're all different?*

   It's true that all customers are different, because all people are different. However, there are some things that nearly all customers want, such as acknowledgement, effort, problem solving, understanding of their needs, efficiency, choices, value, consistency, and confidentiality. While you'll need to tailor your customer service to suit various customers, learning these basics will help you to get it right most of the time.

2. *Customer service is more important when you're dealing face-to-face with a customer than when you're on the phone or the Internet, right?*

   Good customer service is equally important in person, over the phone, or on the Internet. Internet-based businesses have not enjoyed good reputations for customer service in the past, but increasing amounts of attention is being given to this topic, and businesses are beginning to realize that they need to improve in that area.

3. *What should I do if a customer is really angry or upset, or is treating me very rudely?*

   Don't engage with the customer and become angry yourself, first of all. Remember that the customer wants to be acknowledged, to know that you understand his problem, and to be empowered by being given some choices. If you ever feel threatened by a customer or that you're in danger, call someone to help you, or call 911 if no one is around.

07 Setting Up Your Business at Home

Setting up your business in your home can be as simple or as complicated as you choose, but your first step is to locate space you can use as your office. Every office is different. Some are purely utilitarian, while others are elegant. Some are huge and others quite small. I once met an at-home business operator who worked from a closet, and it wasn't even a walk-in closet. It was an ordinary-size clothes closet located in a spare bedroom in his house.

The tricky thing about setting up a business in your home is that you need to work around your family, or whoever else happens to live there. Family members will quickly become resentful if you take over family living space and they can no longer watch their favorite baseball team or reality show on the big-screen TV. If you set up shop on the kitchen table, forcing everyone to find another venue for dinner, you won't win the much-needed support of your family as you get started in your new venture.

If you're lucky, there's a space in your home that's in some way set apart. A writer in Pennsylvania has a great office that was once a screened-in porch. She had the screens replaced with glass, bookshelves built into one wall, and an electric heater installed. The porch already had electricity, but she added a ceiling fan and a good desk lamp, and had a phone line added. It's not a large office, but it's got a door she can close (and even lock if necessary), making it the perfect spot to shut out the rest of the household and write away. Another writer locates her home office on one side of the loft that also serves as a bedroom for her and her husband. It's not as private as the side porch, and she occasionally forces her husband to find another sleeping spot when she works very late, but again, her space is separate from the main living areas of the house, and nicely meets her needs.

A photographer converted the little-used formal living room in his home

Home Office Tip . . .

Size is seldom the critical issue in a home office; it's more about how you make use of the size you have. If you happen to live in a house with several rooms that are not used regularly, your office will sooner or later overflow to occupy all of them. If you live in a studio apartment, your office will have to be the paragon of containment, or you will soon be choked by your equipment, papers, and whatever else you use regularly. Plan and design your office to fit the space you have. Even if you have plenty of space, start as though you don't. It's a good habit to have.

to a studio and happily works away as his wife and kids hang out in the comfortable family room. Clients come in through the front door directly into the studio, while family members use the side door that enters the kitchen.

Be creative and think outside the box when trying to decide where to locate your work space. The guy who worked out of his closet may have been on to something. Is there a little-used walk-in closet in your house? What's going on with your garage? Many people have converted garages, or parts of garages, into living or work space. Some homes have little-used dining rooms set off to the side of the kitchen. Maybe there's a bedroom that used to house a child who now is in college or otherwise living away from home. Is there a room with a big empty corner in it, or a room where empty space could be created? With a little ingenuity and the proper furniture and equipment, it may be possible to set up a home office in a space you'd never thought of.

If you have plenty of space, especially a room that can be dedicated to office use, it's probably best to make it a one-use setup rather than trying to disguise it with some multiuse furniture. This way, you can leave files and papers scattered around, and unfinished tasks don't have to be packed and stored at the end of the day.

A home office should be thought of as more than just a place to work. Sticking to the notion that form follows function may be tempting, but since you will probably spend a lot of time in your home office, I'd suggest that you plan as carefully for its comfort factors as you do for its practicality.

If you prefer a space with few distractions, choose a spot with few windows, where you are less likely to be interrupted by family members. If a view of the outside world is to your liking, your choice is obvious.

Making Sure You're Legal

Every state, county, town, borough, and burg has its own laws governing business use of residential property, and it's very important that you know what they are and adhere to them. Laws pertaining to business use of residential space are different from those that require you to get a business license and register the name of your company. These are regulations specific to the use of your home for business purposes.

Some towns insist that there be a separate exterior door leading directly to your home office, especially if there will be a lot of traffic. Others will insist that you adhere to local parking ordinances that were designed to keep cars from clogging downtown shopping parking spots, not residential areas, but will affect you anyway. Some town ordinances strictly prohibit anyone from running a home office in certain residential zones. Some business owners who live and work in these tightly restricted areas simply keep their work to themselves, figuring that it's nobody else's business if they're making wedding cakes for clients or working as e-bay consultants at home.

Basic Equipment You'll Need to Have

Nearly every business requires equipment that's specific to it. It's difficult to offer piano lessons in your home if you don't have a piano, or work as an eBay consultant if

Home Office Tip . . .

If customers or business associates frequently visit you at your home and it's causing a problem with neighbors, perhaps you can find another location to meet. Many business conversations and meetings take place off hours in restaurants and coffee shops. Just avoid occupying table space at the height of the morning commute, lunch, or dinner hours, and you should be just fine.

If you will be having clients visit you, do whatever is needed to comply with your local ordinances and the anticipated whims of your "friendly" neighbors.

Many municipalities restrict the use of signs in residential areas, so make sure you check on your local regulations before you post a billboard in your front yard announcing your business. The number of employees you're allowed to have may need to be addressed, as well. It's best to err on the side of the law; don't take chances.

you don't have a computer, or create fancy cupcakes if you don't have an oven. Just as you need to have skills that are particular to your business, you're likely to need some equipment that allows you to do what you do. Regardless of what type of business you have, however, it's imperative that you're able to communicate effectively with customers, suppliers, business associates, and others. To that end, let's consider what kind of phone service you'll need.

Telephones

The trend, at least with people 30 or younger, seems to be that telephones are becoming obsolete. Talking on the phone, particularly if it's a land line, appears to be a dying art. It's all text and Twitter and Facebook, with phones more heavily relied upon for messaging and taking pictures than for talking. If you're a young entrepreneur reading this book, however, I strongly advise that you don't give up your phone, and that you have a phone dedicated solely to your business.

It really depends on your personal preference what type of phone you use for what purposes. You might have a land line that's dedicated to your business, and a cell phone that you use for personal use. You might have two cell phones, one for work and one for personal use. You might even have two land lines. However you work it, just remember that trying to consolidate business and personal use in one phone is a prescription for disaster. It not only can make you come off as unprofessional, it erodes on your personal time and life. Many of us have convinced ourselves that we need to be available 24/7, but that's simply not the case. It's great to make sure your customers or clients have a way to get in touch with you if there's some emergency business situation. That's a value-added service you offer them. If it's not an emergency, however, you shouldn't feel obligated to be available at all times. Just make sure that clients who might have emergency situations have a way of getting in touch with you. Cell phones are best used in this case. Pagers seem to be history now.

Fax and Copy Machines

The ability to send just about anything from your computer has decreased dependence on fax machines, but there still is a need for them. You will probably need both a fax machine and a copier, but before you spring for separate units, check out the computer printers that also include copying and faxing functions. You will probably pay less for a multiuse machine than for separate units. Remember, however,

Home Office Tip . . .

It may be different by the time you read this, but as of now, you can't attach your fax to a cell phone. If your business requires heavy use of a fax, you will probably have to have a wired land line.

If you're going with a land line, remember that business lines can be more expensive than residential lines. Unless you want your business listed in the Yellow Pages, however, you may not have to go the business-line route. These rules vary with different phone companies all over the country, and you will have to check this out for yourself. If you choose a residential line for your business, the business name will appear only in the White Pages. This may be all you need.

Even the least expensive telephones have built-in answering capabilities, so separate answering machines (and even answering services) will probably not be necessary. Check your local phone company to see if the line you choose has a call-forwarding service, which directs calls made to your home office line to another site, such as your cell phone. That way you can get business calls when you're on the road without having to give your cell phone number to every customer, supplier, and salesperson you deal with. You also won't have to sort through a bunch of messages when you get back to the office. Phone technology changes rapidly, so it's important that you do your homework to figure out what works best for you. Consider carefully what each carrier has to offer.

if any one of the features quits on you and you have to have the machine repaired, you will be without the other services you probably need to keep your office running. You might consider buying one machine that does faxing and copying, and one that serves as a printer. You will probably have more need for the printer than you will the other machines, and the cost of printers is low enough these days that you're not looking at a big expense.

Here are a few things to keep in mind if you're considering a copier:

- Estimate how many copies you are likely to make in an average month.
- Will you need to collate and staple any of your copies?

- Will you want to copy both sides of any of your work?
- Will you need high-enough resolution to copy art and photos?
- Is color copying an issue?
- Will you have to copy letter-size as well as legal-size documents?
- Will most of your copies be text or images? If you can avoid getting a machine that has all the bells and whistles, you will save a lot on the initial cost as well as the cartridge replacement costs. A simple but high-quality laser printer is often adequate.

Most copiers are pretty durable, but it can cost more to fix one that doesn't work and is out of warranty than it does to buy a new one. The insurance policies the dealers want to sell you are seldom really worth it. If one of these machines is going to quit because of faulty parts or manufacturing, it will probably do so within the standard warranty period. If your business, for some reason, requires making a tremendously high number of copies, you might want to look into leasing a machine instead of buying one. Regardless of whether you lease or buy, be sure to ask about servicing. If you rely on a copier for your business, it's bad news to have it broken down and no technician available to help you.

Fax machines, or the fax features of a combination machine, will probably include more than you really need unless you plan to send a lot of photos, drawings, and documents that include handwriting.

Here are some things to consider before purchasing a fax machine:

- How often will you need to send or receive a document that is only available now as a printed piece of paper? If your printer has scanner capability, chances are that your office computer program includes a subroutine for faxing whatever you can store digitally. You should also be able to receive similar documents and be able to print them on your standard computer printer.
- Will you need capability to send both letter- and legal-size documents?
- Will a stand-alone fax take up space that you could put to better use with something else?

While faxing isn't as common as it used to be, it's still a practical way to send certain types of documents. However, if you can get away with a printer that has a scanner and use the fax program that came with your computer's office program,

I'd suggest that you go this route. As your business grows, you will probably have to adjust your thinking about fax machines, copiers, and printers. Each of these devices is a lot less expensive than they were just a few short years ago, and you may find that your needs change as your business advances.

The One Machine You Can't Do Without

No, it's not the coffeemaker (although that certainly may qualify as the appliance you can't do without)—it's the computer! But you already knew that, right? There's hardly a businessperson left who can survive without a computer—it's as plain as that. The real question becomes: Will you work with an office PC and a separate laptop for work in the field, or should you consider buying one of the heavy-duty laptops that can serve you well both in the office and in the field? Alternately, PDAs such as Palm Pilots, iPhones, iPacs, MyPals, and Blackberries can nicely serve as portable computers, so you might choose to splurge on something fun like one of those, and leave the computer in the office.

It can be risky to rely solely on one computer. Having two computers of some sort means that you can back up all your stuff so it's present on both machines. A relatively inexpensive PC and similar laptop will probably cost about the same, or possibly a little more than one good heavy-duty portable machine. Having two means that you will always be able to work while one is being fixed. It also means that your data can be backed up quickly and available immediately on both machines.

A crash on one machine means that the original software package must be reinstalled in the repaired machine and that all the backed-up data must be installed. Most backup programs handle only data, not programs you may have installed yourself. By keeping two machines in complete sync, you are ready to go without all the fuss if one bites the dust.

If you're pinching pennies, and it seems that most people are these days, and you don't want to invest in a new backup laptop, pick up a used machine and have a pro go over it and bring it up to speed. You'll save about half of what you'd pay for a new laptop, and you'll get the opportunity to extend some business to a home-based computer repair guy!

You can choose from a huge number of machines and almost as many different computer manufacturers. Again, it's important that you do your homework carefully, as you and your business are likely to be very dependent on your computer system.

Buy New or Upgrade?

The answer to the question of whether you should buy all new computer equipment or hang on to what you have and upgrade as you can depends on a couple of factors, namely, capabilities and finances. Your first chore is to assess whether your current computer has the capabilities that your new business will require. If so, you just might be smart to hold onto it for a while. Just because a computer is old is not a good reason to abandon it. I've been told that most computers and other electronic

Home Office Tip . . .

Don't throw away or give away your old computer when you upgrade to a new one. As long as it is working and will handle the software you plan to use on a new machine, keep the clunker as a backup. If it's slow, chances are that it's because you have pretty much crammed your hard drive with stuff you either never used or used only occasionally. Think about reformatting the hard drive on your old machine to get rid of all the clutter and installing only the programs you use for your business. Keep your Internet connection software, of course; once you've cleaned the junk off your hard drive, you'll be surprised at how fast it will run.

As long as your computer is working well, is fast enough to do what you want it to do, and has the storage capability you need, stick with it. The things that usually call for upgrade can be handled with investing in another printer. If your computer is capable of handling upgraded software such as a new operating system or any of the programs you use routinely, you should be okay. And when you run out of memory, you can either install new memory boards in the machine, or you can pick up a new external hard drive for around a hundred bucks that can possibly give you even more storage capacity than you have in the onboard memory. So, it boils down to speed, memory, and the ability to run newer software efficiently.

Having said this, however, even, or maybe especially, when you're on a tight budget, you should always keep your eye out for bargains. Being forced to buy a new computer because your old one died leaves you are at the mercy of pricing available at that moment. When new models are being introduced, and after holidays when computers are often given as gifts, you can usually pick up some very good bargains.

office equipment will fail early on if they are going to fail at all. And in most cases your warranty will probably cover the cost of repair or replacement. Once a machine has had its shakedown cruise, it will probably last longer than you want it to. That is, it will keep on working when you really want to upgrade to the new super name laptop that's a lot more fun than your hardworking, faithful desktop.

Peripherals and Software

Most computers today are pretty much self-contained. That is, they have built-in modems, multiple USB ports, and Ethernet connections. The software that accompanies most new computers is usually just right for a start-up consulting business. You will probably be given the choice of a home or professional version of Word. The professional version is quite a bit more expensive than the home version, and it may be that you just don't need it.

If you plan to use some heavy-duty programs for graphics or other purposes, make sure it will run on your machine. If you have a new machine that has only ESB ports, but you have some older peripheral hardware that requires an RS232 port, there are simple in-line adapters you can buy for under $20 that will allow you to use older externally connected hardware.

Simply because your computer may have a bunch of USB ports, don't hook up everything you own to them. The more software-driven peripherals you have attached, the slower your machine will run. Remember: One of the big advantages of USB ports is that they allow you to add and remove hardware without having to shut down, connect, and reboot as was necessary with the older serial ports. Keep your machine lean and mean!

Most computers are sold today with flat-screen displays. I still see some machines offered with CRT displays, however. Just remember that the flat screen display takes up a lot less space and it uses considerably less power than does a CRT display.

The Internet

It's safe to say that you probably won't be able to do business unless you have an Internet connection and can use it efficiently and effectively. It's well beyond the scope of this book to bring you up to speed on the Internet. There's plenty of help available from books, friends, or courses at local continuing education programs.

Most Internet connections today are made through high-speed connections to your telephone line or wireless connections, which hook you into cable and satellite connections. You can even still get on via a slow dial-up connection, but why would you want to? Armed with a Wi-Fi-enabled laptop, you should be able to access the Internet without needing to make any wired connection from just about every location in the country.

We'll get back to the Internet in chapter 11, as it also serves as a valuable marketing tool. It's not only the fastest way to communicate, but it's also becoming one of the better ways to get the word out about your business and attract new customers.

Furniture and Lighting

While's it's important to have the right equipment to allow you to communicate and generate work and reports, keep records, and complete other business tasks, office furniture is something you might be able to go easy on, at least at first. Many a home office has been started with little more than a table or desk, a filing cabinet or two, a chair, and a light. Remember that if you're strapped for cash and don't want to finance a bunch of stuff, you can always find quality furniture for sale secondhand at used furniture stores and auction houses.

You may end up with a beautiful, solid wood desk for less than you'd pay for a cheapie at the office supply store. Of the furniture you need, the chair and lights are arguably the most important. If your business requires you to spend long hours sitting at a desk or in front of a computer, the chair you choose is vitally important. Make sure it's ergonomic, which means it will support your lower back and promote good posture.

Don't be tempted to buy a chair that looks great, but is awful to sit in. Starting your own business requires that you be on top of your game, not confined to bed with an aching back.

Oh, My Aching Back!

The American Chiropractic Association reports that 80 percent of all Americans suffer from back problems at some point of their lives, and that back pain is on one of the most common reasons for missed work. Most back problems, experts say, are not caused by any serious condition, but by factors such as improper posture or seating.

Lighting is the other big deal when furnishing your home office. Having the proper lighting is imperative for your health and comfort. If you have to strain to see what you're doing because you don't have adequate lighting, you're just asking to end up with a headache. Hopefully, your office gets lots of natural light, which tends to make it more cheerful and inviting. If you don't have natural light, try to not have to rely (at least not solely) on overhead lighting. Make sure you have a good desk light with the proper bulb.

You'll also need some storage space for files, books, manuals, correspondence, and other purposes. We are still a long way from achieving the paperless society that's been predicted for years, so you'll need some filing cabinets and perhaps some book shelves to help keep you organized and your office tidy. And, don't forget little items like a large trash can, desk organizer, and bulletin board.

Stationery, Business Cards, Letterhead, and Other Printed Material

Even though most of your communicating will probably be done by way of the Internet and telephone, the need for stationery and business cards still exists. With the right software and printer, you can not only design and print everything you will need, but you can do it on demand rather than having to buy and store boxes of letterhead and envelopes. You can also create your own business cards, which you can print out onto perforated sheets of paper. If you choose to make your own stationary and cards, just be sure that they look professional. You might consider seeking the services of a home-based designer to help you achieve the look you want.

If you do go it along, here are a few tips to keep you from looking like a total amateur:

- Keep the logo, if you use one, simple. Professional designers will tell you all about the importance of simplicity and functionality.
- Don't try to tell a long story on your card or letterhead.
- Stay away from using a lot of color, which can result in a gaudy look.
- Choose a simple, uncomplicated, and easy-to-read typeface.
- Look at the letterheads of some of the major consulting firms in your field and you will quickly see that glitz is not the way to go.
- Avoid the urge to "stand out" by doing something "different" with your company graphics. Your graphics should resemble those of the established firms in your field without actually copying them.

The Importance of Privacy

While working at home has many advantages, which were discussed earlier, keeping your work and family life separate can be a huge challenge. If you can, locate your office in as private a location as possible, and set some boundaries with other who reside in the home. You might establish times when, every couple of hours, you check in to see what's going on, or you take a lunch break, or you're available to drive someone to an appointment. Insist, though, that you are left alone when you need to be, and not constantly interrupted. Privacy is particularly important if your business requires customers or clients to visit you in your office. If that's the case, a private entrance is really desirable. If a private entrance isn't an option, and your client isn't going to be impressed by the sight of a teenager lying on the couch in the middle of the afternoon, be sure the entry way to your office is clear at the time the client is expected.

Working from your home requires everyone who lives in the house to be on board. You actually might consider working up an agreement and having everyone sign it, pledging to adhere to rules that are necessary for you to work uninterrupted and professionally.

While privacy is important, security is even more so. If you store private records or documents in your office, make sure it's locked at all times when you're not there. Leaving private files open could jeopardize your business, or even have legal implications.

Frequently Asked Questions

1. *How big of an investment will I need to make when setting up my home office?*

   Your investment will depend largely on what you need. If your business requires a lot of special equipment, you'll need to come up with a lot more funding than if you just need the basic desk, chair, phone, and reliable computer system. You can make your office as basic or deluxe as you want, but you should remember that it's usually best to start off with what you really need and add to and upgrade as your business expands. Don't overlook secondhand furniture and refurbished electronic equipment if money is tight, as it usually is for someone just starting out.

2. *What do I do on an occasion when I need more space or privacy than my home office allows, perhaps for an important meeting with a potential client or clients?* You have a couple of options. You could invite the client to lunch and discuss the matter there. Or, you could look into shared offices that are available in many cities and some other communities. A shared office that is well run and staffed can be an excellent adjunct to a home office. Many of these services have conference room space that, when booked in advance, can be used for client meetings and they provide excellent office backup.

3. *My home office is not in a house, but in my condominium. The bylaws only talk about office and professional signage, mainly because there are doctors' offices on the lower floors. Although no one has complained, should I let the association know that I work from my home office?* If there are no specific prohibitions stated in your condominium agreement, just leave it alone; continue to be a good unit owner and neighbor.

Managing Your Business Finances

Home-based business owners, and certainly other business owners, as well, sometimes tend to separate the financial aspects of their businesses from the other parts. Many entrepreneurs thrive on the day-to-day operations of the business, and managing employees, and screening potential clients, and strategizing about how to improve their marketing efforts. And, of course, all business owners like to see checks coming in. For some reason, however, many business owners seem resistant to paying close attention to the bookkeeping and recordkeeping tasks that are integral to keeping the businesses successful.

You read back in chapter 2 that you need to have an accountant, and how to go about finding a good one. That hasn't changed. You still need an accountant, even if your business is a sole proprietorship and you're the only employee. Remember the factors for which an accountant is necessary; obtaining financial advice you need to start your business, registering your business for tax purposes and other tax issues, reviewing the financial portion of your business plan, and so forth and so on. In addition, if you need to have financial reports prepared for a third party, such as a banker, often, the third party will request that the reports come from an accountant. Every business person should have an accountant, and, if you're fortunate enough to find a good one who you like early on in your business life, consider yourself lucky. One of the joys of owning your own business is cultivating professional relationships over time.

That doesn't mean, however, that you'll rely on an accountant for the day-to-day financial matters of your business. That, indeed, would be cost prohibitive and is totally unnecessary. It's your responsibility as the owner of your business to be hands-on with the financials. Even if you hire a part-time bookkeeper or someone to help you with the financial end of the business, or you decide to outsource bookkeeping and payroll tasks, it's imperative that you know at all times what's going on with all aspects of your business, especially money. Keeping accurate financial records is the only way you're going to have a realistic overview of how your business is doing, and there are some very good accounting software programs to help you do that. Are you making money or losing it? Is it clear sailing ahead, or are you looking toward financial trouble down the road? Keeping good financial records, and keeping up with them, will help you stay on top of your situation and give you early warning if something is your finances are getting off track.

In this chapter, we'll look at methods of keeping track of finances and managing your money, as well as business software that can make it easier for you, and other aspects of managing your business finances. Let's get started.

Why Are Good Financial Records So Important?

There are lots of reasons why it's important to keep good financial records, some of which you just read. Let's spend a little more time thinking about that, however, as it is fundamental to the success of your business.

Accurate, up-to-date records allow you make well informed financial-related decisions. How can you know how much inventory you can order if you're not sure how much available cash you have? How do you know if you should agree to contract with a particular client if you have no idea if you were paid for the last three jobs you did? Lacking complete and accurate financial records, or not making the effort to keep on top of those records, puts you at a real disadvantage when it comes to making any sort of decision, because your decision won't be an informed one.

If you need to borrow money for your business or are looking to obtain capital for expansion or another reasons, lenders are going to be much more impressed when you present an organized overview of your financial situation than a sloppy, incomplete one. Even if you have your accountant help you prepare the information, it will be based on the records you've kept over the course of doing business.

Good financial records will help you to budget and plan for the future of your business. A business budget, just like a personal budget, can help you to control expenditures and keep your finances on track.

Tax season rolls around every year, and, regardless of the type of business you have, you're going to need sound financial records to hand over to your accountant so that your tax returns can be prepared. If your accountant needs to sort through inaccurate or incomplete financial records, you can be sure that it's going to result in a higher bill for his services than if the records were neat and complete.

Any business that has any employees must comply with federal and state payroll tax rules, which can be complex. You need to be aware of deadlines in order to avoid penalties, provide W-2 forms for employees, and be in compliance in other ways, as well. If your payroll and other financial records are incomplete or you can't make sense out them, it's going to be very difficult to adhere to all the regulations. You even need to have good financial records in order to figure out how much to pay yourself.

If your business is a partnership or corporation you'll need good records to figure out the amounts of profit to distribute to each partner or shareholder.

Those are just a few reasons why good record keeping is essential to a healthy business—there are others. So, remember, whether you're keeping the records yourself, or hiring someone to keep them for you, it's really, really important to make sure they're accurate and that you know what's in them.

Accounting 101

Before you can start keeping good financial records, you've got to have an understanding of basic accounting. If you're finding the basic level of this text to make for slow reading, or even to be insulting, still take time to skim over it, and understand that, while you may have graduated from college with a business degree or have business financial experience, many entrepreneurs do not. There's a breed of entrepreneurs who begin very young, or come into the entrepreneurial field from another career, with a great idea and the ability to get their hands on some start-off money, and they run with it, learning all things business as they go. And, lacking a basic understanding of accounting and basic business systems can lead entrepreneurs into perilous territory. So, on we go.

Accounting is simply the procedure of gathering, processing, and reporting on the financial information that affects your company. On a very basic level, there are two accounting methods: cash and accrual. If you use the cash method of accounting, you only record income when you actually receive it from a customer or client—when it's in hand. And, you record payment at the time that you make it, as soon as you hand over the cash or write the check or swipe a debit card. Cash accounting is the easiest method, because it keeps track of only cash in and cash out. The problem, though, is that businesses, even small ones, which rely solely on cash are few and far between. Most businesses buy and sell on credit, meaning that there's money in and out that's floating around for a while before it actually lands in the till or shows up as an expense. For that reasons, most businesses use the accrual method of accounting, with which every transaction gets recorded as it happens, whether or not there was an exchange of cash. This method gives you a better overview of your financial picture because it can track profits and losses.

Regardless of which accounting method you use, the process of accounting works like this.

A business transaction occurs, meaning that someone buys something from you, or you buy something from someone else. The sale is recorded with a sales invoice or a check, receipt, or some other document.

The business transaction is recorded into a journal, which can be kept by hand or with accounting software.

Journal entries are then recorded in a general ledger, which is a collection of balance sheet, income, and expense records used in the business's accounting system. The journal entries are grouped by the type of transaction, and which account each transaction affects.

At the end of an accounting period, all of the account balances in the general ledger are added up to get a trial balance. The sum of the debit balances has to be equal to the sum of the credit balances. If they're not equal, there's something wrong and you need to go back over everything to determine what it is.

The information in the trial balance is prepared and financial statements are issued.

Another accounting decision you'll need to consider is whether to use a single-entry or double-entry account system. A double-entry system, which means that every transaction has both a credit and a debit entry, is the more commonly used system and is recommended because it gives you a system of checks and balances. If you use a software program, it provides an automatic double entry system. You make the entry on either the credit or debit side, and the software will automatically enter it on the other. This provides a system of checks and balances and helps you to be able to find mistakes more easily.

Keeping Track of Your Daily Transactions

Understanding how a basic accounting system works is great, but if you don't know what you're keeping track of, it won't do you much good at all. As the owner of a home-based business, you've got to carefully record the sales, purchases, and any other transactions that occur on a day-to-day basis. You'll need to understand and keep track of:

- Sales and revenue transactions. Daily sales and revenues can be recorded in a sales journal, or, for convenience, use a journal that combines sales and cash receipts.
- Cash transactions. This sounds obvious, but there are different kinds of cash transactions that get recorded in different places.
- Accounts payable, which is the money you need to pay what you owe to others. Maybe you owe money to vendors or suppliers, or are making payments a piece of equipment you bought. You should keep a separate ledger account for everyone you owe so you know exactly where you stand.
- Accounts receivable are the monies owed to you. You should keep a separate list for each customer on which you note accounts receivable.
- Summaries of transactions are recorded in the general ledger, which is the place you begin to organize your financial statements.

The Basics of Financial Statements

There are three basic forms of financial statements: the income statement, balance sheet, and cash flow analysis. Most business owners have their accountants prepare financial statements, but some prepare them themselves. Whether or not you do your own or leave it to your accountant, these are important documents that you should understand and be familiar with. What follows in this section are brief overviews of these three types of financial statements, but there is much more to know and understand about them than what you'll read here. You can find a lot more information from the Small Business Administration (www.sba.gov) and other business-based sites. You also can download templates of financial statements so you can see what they look like and get a feel for how to use them. Let's start with the income statement.

The Income Statement

Sometimes called a profit-and-loss statement, the income statement tells you whether or not your business is profitable. It adds up your revenues, or the monies that you've made, and then subtracts what you had to spend to make the revenues. The result, assuming that it's positive, is your profit.

So, let's say that your home-based business buys and sells handcrafted baskets. You hire four people who weave baskets, and you sell them on the Internet and to a network of specialty shops and gift shops. You sell every basket for $50, and you pay $30 for each one. That means that your gross profit is $20 on each basket.

However, you don't get to keep $20 for each basket sold, because there are expenses associated with selling them. If you have employees helping you you've got to pay them, you pay to advertise the baskets, you have to pay insurance, buy office supplies, pay taxes, shipping costs, and so forth and so on. When you add up all those costs and divide them by the number of baskets sold, you have to deduct that amount from your gross profit. So, if it turns out that all your expenses added together and divided by the number of baskets sold comes to $5 per basket, you have to subtract that amount from your gross profit. This gives you your net income.

Your expenses can be broken down into two categories: cost of sales expenses and operating expenses. Cost of sales expenses also are called cost of goods sold, and they are the cost of the baskets. If you ran a basket-making factory, your cost of sales expenses would include your costs for raw materials and all the other expenses necessary to produce the baskets. Your operating expenses are the monies that you spend running your business, such as salaries, utility costs, insurance, rent, and so forth.

Most businesses prepare year-end income statements, but they can be done at any time interval, such as quarterly or even monthly.

The Balance Sheet

The balance sheet, on which is listed all your assets and liabilities, gives you an overview of your business finances. A balance sheet also is known as a statement of financial position, because it tells you where you stand financially at a particular point of time. Balance sheets often are referred to as snapshots, as they capture your financial situation at a given time.

The difference between your assets and your liabilities is called your owner's equity, or net worth. It's what's left over after the liabilities have been subtracted from the assets, and it's the number that you want to maximize as much as possible because it affects the value of your business.

The balance sheet contains three parts: assets, liabilities, and ownership equity. The asset section contains current assets, which are any assets than can easily be converted into cash. These would include: cash and petty cash, land, buildings, vehicles, office supplies, furniture, equipment, accounts receivable, bank accounts, prepaid rent, prepaid expenses, prepaid insurance, inventory, investments, and reserve for bad debts.

Liabilities would include anything that needed to be paid or anything that is payable, such as accounts, interest, salaries, dividends, taxes, mortgage payments, rent, and loans.

Balance sheets are based on the following accounting equation: *net worth must equal asset minus liabilities*. If you're just getting your business started and don't yet have assets and liabilities, you can do a personal balance sheet just for fun and to get an idea of how it works. Once your business is up and running and you've got a balance sheet, you should review it regularly so you can keep up with what's happening financially in your business.

Cash Flow Analysis

A cash flow analysis is important because it indicates your ability to pay bills and cover expenses. It tracks the money coming into your business, which, as you no doubt know, is critical to new business owners.

While your income statement focuses on earnings from operations, the cash flow analysis takes into consideration investments, repayment of loans, money you've borrowed, and other changes that show up on your balance sheet. The cash flow analysis helps you see ahead of time when you might start to run out of cash with which to cover expenses, and allows you to plan how you'll solve that problem, either by borrowing money or cutting back on the expenses.

Because cash flow is so important to your business, timely payment on the part of your customers is very important. Some new business owners are reluctant to bill in full, or to follow up on late payments, but these are aspects of owning your own business that you'll need to handle. Most businesses have periods during which they are busier than others, with more money coming in. But, remember that if you let a customer who's in a slow period off the hook by allowing her to delay payment, you're putting yourself in the same situation. Keep an eye on your cash flow analysis and nicely, but firmly, remind slow-paying customers of their obligation. If you're going to have trouble collecting payments from a customer, it's best to find out early on in your business relationship.

Getting the Most from Your Financial Statements

Once you've taken the time and made the effort to get good financial statements, make sure that you use them to your advantage. Your income statement will help you to be able to gauge what your expenses and sales will be at the end of the year, giving you a picture of where you stand month to month. You'll be able to tell whether you're on track or not, or whether you need to beef up sales or cut back on expenses.

The balance sheet also can help you to better manage your business's financial system by providing a big picture scenario of where you are. If you're planning on making a major purchase or paying off some loans, you can create a projected balance sheet for the coming year to help you get an idea of what it will look like after your purchase or debt reduction.

You can use your last year's cash flow analysis as a predictor to your sales and expenses for the current year. If last year's analysis shows a two-month slump in July and August, you might want to anticipate a similar slump for the same period in the current year, and perhaps adjust your marketing plan in an effort to generate extra business during those months. A past analysis can help you to compare last year's and this year's sales and expenses and challenge you to better your company's financial situation month by month.

Closing the Books

When you get to the end of an accounting period, you'll need to "close the books." You have to do this at least once a year in order to file your income tax return, but for some businesses it's a good idea to close out the books more frequently, perhaps monthly, every other month, or quarterly.

So, what does it mean to "close the books?" Closing the books is simply the transfer of account balances into the general ledger at the end of an accounting period.

Closing your books makes it easier to perform tasks such as sending out customer statements, preparing state sales tax reports, paying suppliers, and reconciling your bank statement.

Choosing Accounting Software

There are dozens of accounting software programs marketed to small businesses, and, if you have time, you can spend hours and hours researching and trying to decide which one you would most like to use. If you don't have unlimited time to spend deciding which program to get, read the descriptions below and then research further the ones that seem to make the most sense for your business. You can find all kinds of information about accounting software on line, or go to an authoritative source such as:

- Intuit QuickBooks Accounting Software. QuickBooks is a very popular accounting and payroll program designed for small businesses. It comes in the following editions: Basic, Online, Pro, and Premier. While the Basic Edition includes enough features for many small businesses, the Pro Edition comes with bells and whistles including a vehicle mileage tracker and cash flow projector.

- Sage BusinessVision Accounting Software. Available in Limited, Small Business, Standard, and Client Server editions, Sage BusinessVision has been praised for features which complete accounting automatically. One review pointed out that year-end processing is automatic, allowing you to continue to apply backdated transactions to the previous year, even after year-end. And, an add-on feature offers a fully integrated e-commerce Web store and shopping cart.

- Microsoft Office Small Business Accounting. This program is especially popular with users of Microsoft Office because it allows you to reuse data already entered into Excel or Outlook, and offers integration with the Business Contact Manager that makes it easy to stay on top of accounts. A range of add-on features allow you to perform tasks ranging from online payroll to PayPal invoicing. The program is praised as being one of the most easy to use, while containing robust features.

- Simply Accounting Software. Simply Accounting is praised as containing all the reports and features that any small business needs, including Internet and e-commerce features. The program is easy to learn, thanks to screen tips and functional drag and drop features, and comes multi-user ready. Features of the professional versions include time and billing modules.

- Peachtree Complete Accounting Software. This program includes more than 125 reports and features, including in-depth inventory, time and billing, and job costing. It comes multi-user ready, and also is available in Premium and First Accounting versions. Peachtree's database forms for customers, vendors, and inventory items are praised as being more flexible than those of its competitors, with equally adaptable transaction forms. Its time-billing section, inventory capability, and payroll solutions features also have been heralded.

Accounting software is available in office supply stores, electronics stores, mail order houses and directly from software publishers. You should check with your accountant before buying software to make sure what you will be using is compatible with his system. If you have employees who will be using the system, look for one with passwords that control access to select transactions. It's important to have restricted access to your accounting records to protect both you and your employees.

Frequently Asked Questions

1. *I'm trying to be very careful about how much money I need to spend to get my business up and running. I have a little bit of experience with finances, and I'm thinking of not hiring an accountant in order to save the costs. Is there any reason I need an accountant right away?*

    The old saying, "a little knowledge is a dangerous thing," may very well be applicable in your situation. While it's likely that, with the help of some business accounting software, you won't have much trouble with your day-to-day business finances, you still should plan on hiring an accountant as you get your business underway. You'll need financial advice when getting your business established, and business taxes are complicated enough that you'll want to have an accountant available to help you with them. Also, if your banker or another third party requires financial reports concerning

---

your business, the third party may insist that an accountant prepares the reports. Establish a relationship with a good accountant now, and you'll reap the benefits for a long time to come.

2. *What's the difference between financial statements and financial analysis? Don't financial statements provide an analysis of a business's financial situation?*

   Financial statements provide information about the financial situation, performance, and changes within a business, and a financial analysis is a study of that information to provide a thorough understanding of what the statements mean. Business finance can be complicated, and the bigger your business gets the more attention you'll need to give to it, another reason why it's important to have an accountant you know and trust.

09 Taxes and the Home-Based Business

One of the most compelling reasons people choose to work from home is the idea that tax deductions can greatly diminish the cost of operating the house they live and work in. Maybe "greatly" isn't the best word, but those deductions can make a difference, especially when you are just starting out. However, unless you know what can and cannot be included in your list of deductions, you may be invited to have a chat with the tax man.

This chapter is basically a summary of what you can and cannot do in your office and your living quarters and still expect to reduce your taxes substantially. And—please keep this in mind—tax laws change all the time. It's probably a safe assumption that current economic conditions will result in tax regulations changing even faster and more dramatically than they have in the past. Don't get nervous! Most of the changes probably will favor you and won't add much to your tax burden.

The thrust of this chapter is to give you an overall picture of what is now possible, how you can benefit from the current laws, and what you have to do to comply. Bear in mind that whatever you do, it's critical to document everything. If you have selected an accountant and set up a computer-based financial management system, you should already have a general idea of what you can and cannot do, and how to handle everything.

Good recordkeeping is critical. You will have to record all expenses that allow you to modify your taxes, and you also want to have the kind of records that tell you whether you are in good or bad shape, and what you can do about it in either case.

There are no worksheets included in this chapter because no two businesses are the same, and no two will have identical financial and tax-reporting needs. As you go through this chapter, you should be able to spot the points that will work for you. Your own checklist will become self-evident. It will then be a matter of plugging everything into the system you are using, or the one your accountant sets up, and then going after the business you need.

One more note before you dig into this chapter: Reading about taxes and paperwork can be a little depressing, so we've taken the liberty of lacing this chapter with comments from people you might recognize and who might provide you with a much-needed laugh.

Deductions and Regulations for the Home-Based Business

One of the most attractive features of working from home, other than the short commute, is that you can deduct some significant home expenses from your personal income tax. But your accountant will warn you not to go overboard. If a random audit spots an irregularity on your tax return, it's likely to result in the one thing that is worse than the dreaded blue screen of death that signals a crash on your computer—an audit! So don't put Uncle Charlie on your payroll when you know full well he still lives with Momma three thousand miles away and doesn't have a clue about a your business.

It turns out that your home office doesn't actually need to be in a home. According to the current tax regs, if your office has space for cooking, sleeping, and working, it could be a rented house, a house you own, a motor home, a boat, condo, co-op apartment, or maybe even a tent. A tax consultant/writer lived with his wife on a sailboat. In summer they berthed in the Norfolk, Virginia, area, and they spent winters in southern Florida. Talk about an enviable home office!

Just so you know, regulations can differ for a business operated outside of the house. This is a detail you will need to clear up after meeting with your accountant.

Before you begin slashing away at your current taxes, let's take a look at the tax laws that apply to a home business:

- The space you use for your business must be used exclusively for your business.
- The office space must be in regular use; occasional use won't cut it. Your home office must be where you work regularly.
- The office must be your prime location. If you must have other locations in order to serve remote clients, they will not qualify for the tax deduction.

If you meet with clients regularly, this must be the place where you would meet. You probably wouldn't be nailed if you occasionally rented other sites for special meeting and occasions, but your home must serve as your main site for client and customer contact.

These are the key elements of the regulations. However, this presents only the broad picture; you should read the regulations yourself, or ask your accountant for her take on your proposed use. For example, some local governments require that a home office have separate outside entries for clients and a separate bathroom for employees. This may have no bearing on taxes, but while you are getting the tax advice from your accountant, ask about these requirements, too.

The first thing the tax folks look for is multiple use of the space. If you write client reports on a desk in the corner of your bedroom, forget about a tax deduction. Don't even think about writing off your swimming pool just because you let John Jones take a dip while you finished repairing his computer. You can probably get away with writing off some space that is used exclusively for record storage as long as you can show that you do not have sufficient storage space in the home office itself.

Direct and Indirect Expenses

Before you get carried away, don't have the house painted and expect that the IRS will look favorably on your deduction of the entire bill from your federal taxes. The IRS is very picky about how you define the space that directly relates to your business, and that which doesn't come close. And they are just as picky about how you define direct, indirect, and unrelated expenses. *Direct expenses* are those which are directly related to the business use of your home office. Painting your home office is a direct expense and can be used as a deduction, but painting the entire house and trying to convince an IRS agent that it's necessary to impress your customers won't

---

Lighten Up . . .

ALBERT EINSTEIN: "The hardest thing in the world to understand is the income tax."
ARTHUR GODFREY: "I'm proud to be paying taxes in the U.S. The only thing is, I could be just as proud for half the money."
JAY LENO: "Worried about an IRS audit? Avoid what's called a red flag. That's something the IRS always looks for. For example, say you have some money left over in your bank account after paying taxes. That's a red flag."

work. Direct expenses are fully deductible, but don't get carried away. You can't deduct more than the gross income that your home office produces. The IRS wants you to be serious about your business and not just playing at it in order to claim a tax deduction.

Indirect expenses include such items as utilities, insurance, and repairs. These deductions are calculated on a proportional basis. For example, if you use 15 percent of your total home area for business, you are only permitted to deduct 15 percent of the cost of your homeowner's insurance policy. Unrelated expenses include items that you would have a tough time justifying to the IRS, such as garden maintenance. You can try, but better hope that your IRS auditor has a sense of humor. I've been told the interviews can be pretty intense.

The direct expenses are usually pretty obvious; it's the indirect expenses that get most people in trouble. Let's look at some of the indirect expenses a consultant working from a home office might be able to use for tax breaks.

Insurance

Whether you own your home or rent it, if you carry a homeowner's insurance policy on the property, you can deduct an amount equivalent to the percentage of the space you use for your home office. Most people who work from home offices usually carry additional policies which cover things their home policy might not cover. The cost of the additional policies is better treated as a direct expense for tax purposes. Shop for the best policies, even though the money you save might not be worth the time you spend comparison shopping. Just a thought!

Security

You can deduct a portion of the cost of a home security system based on your percentage of use, and there is even a depreciation allowance for your equipment. Again, if you have a system separate from your home system, it's probably best to treat the cost as a direct expense to the business, and not as a deduction based on the cost of a system which protects the rest of your home.

Rent and Mortgage Payments

Here's where people get in the most trouble. The IRS sees rent and mortgage payments as personal expenses, and most personal expenses are not deductible. However, if you rent a home and use a portion of that home for your business office, the rental is considered an indirect expense and is deductible. If you own your home, don't even think about trying to deduct what might be the going rental rate from your taxes. The IRS doesn't smile on those who think of themselves as landlords and tenants simultaneously. It is possible, however, to claim depreciation on that part of the office in the home that you own.

Repairs

Most repairs that are necessary and have an immediate impact on the operation of your office will qualify for a tax deduction. However, you must still consider the percentage-of-use factor. For example, if your home air conditioner gives up and your office is cooled by this system, the amount you can claim will still be based on the percentage of the total space the office occupies. If your office has a window air conditioner that has no effect on the rest of the house, that repair will be deductible. If any significant repairs are needed, you will probably have to depreciate the cost, so check with your accountant before you spend the money.

Property Taxes

If local regulations permit you to have a home office, you can deduct the appropriate percentage from your taxes.

Moving Costs

If local regulations permit a home office, the appropriate portion of the cost of a move can be deducted.

Other Tax Deductions

While it would be a mistake to not take advantage of some of the other tax deductions that are available, it would be an even bigger mistake to try to take advantage of every tax break. You'd never get any work done. Just remember that everything you claim must be documented with careful and detailed records.

Your accountant will be able to give you the advice you need on which tax breaks are worthwhile and which ones are not. Her list will be based specifically on your particular business. For example, if you use Internet services for both business and personal reasons, you can only deduct the time you spend online doing business as a business expense. If your online business time is extensive, your accountant might suggest that you record it and pro-rate it for tax purposes. For anyone else, that kind of minutiae would be mind-numbing and counterproductive. So, with this in mind, here's a list of questions and answers for you to consider.

Q. One of my customers moved out of town without paying me for the (expensive) catering job I'd done for her. I've been unable to contact her or even find out where she went. Can this be deducted as a bad debt?

A. If you operate on a cash basis, as most home-based businesses do, you can't do this. If you had loaned the client some money, the debt would be deductible. On the other hand, if you operate on an accrual basis and had already reported the debt as income, it would not qualify. There has to be an actual loss of money to qualify.

Q. My one computer is used for home as well as business. Can I deduct any of the cost for business use?

A. If you can clearly document the business-related use, you can deduct the business portion of the cost. There are two ways you can do this, and it's best to get advice from your accountant regarding which would be of more benefit to you for your particular business. Your accountant should be able to explain the hobby-loss regulation in fewer words than it would take here. And, besides, we're probably talking about peanuts anyway.

Q. Are sales taxes on products and supplies I buy for my business deductible?

A. You can deduct sales taxes on supplies, but you can't deduct sales taxes on capital assets you purchase. Your accountant will tell you how to capitalize the sales tax on the cost of any taxable assets you purchase.

Q. What is the difference between a business expense and a business asset?

A. For tax purposes, a *business asset* is something of value you acquire which you plan to use in your business for more than one year. Tangible things such as computers and intangible things such as patents are, then, assets. A *business expense* is money spent on products and some services to be used in the current tax year. For tax purposes, *business expenses* can be deducted immediately from income. You will have to spread out the cost of an asset, and it must be deducted over more than a year. Don't guess here; if you are in doubt about how to classify something, ask your accountant. You could find yourself three or four years later having to explain your reasoning to the IRS, and possibly paying back taxes as well as some interest and penalties.

Q. What about business-travel expenses?

A. If the main purpose of the trip is business-related, there is a lot you can deduct from your taxes. For example, you can deduct train fare and airfare, hotel room charges, and even some of the incidentals such as laundry, cab fare, car rental, and phone calls. You can only deduct half of your meal costs and your costs to entertain a client. There's a lot more, so play it safe and ask your accountant for her advice on the items that are currently deductible.

Q. Suppose I plan to visit some clients while on vacation with my family; what portion of those expenses are deductible?

A. The best advice I can give you, given the space available in this book, is to check with your accountant. While many of the expenses are deductible, it gets complex, so you should check with your accountant to be sure. Be sure to document everything and keep all records and receipts.

Warning!

The few questions you have just read only scratch the surface, and are included mainly because they seem to be the questions most people ask when they have never before had a business or worked from home. As important as it may seem to you to get as many tax deductions as you can, you could find yourself spending more time documenting purchases and activities than you should.

Just as important as knowing what you can deduct from your taxes is knowing what the IRS requires in terms of reporting your business financials. Failure to comply with many of the regulations will not only require you to pay what you might owe the IRS, but potentially interest payments and fines as well.

Business author Grace W. Weinstein suggests that you keep copies of your filed tax returns forever, and that you hold on to all papers that even remotely relate to your home expenses for at least five years after you may sell the house. She also feels it's important to keep canceled checks and receipts substantiating tax deductions for at least three years after the filing date, since the IRS has three years from the filing deadline to audit your federal return—unless you fail to report 25 percent of your income. In that case, the IRS has six years to mount a challenge. File a fraudulent return—or don't file at all—and you're fair game forever.

Storing and Retention of Records

What You Can Store on the Computer

If you use an accountant and that accountant uses a data-based accounting system, most of the critical financial records and numbers will be filed on the program database. Since computers have been known to eat data from time to time, it makes sense to count on more than the memory in your hard drive for these records. Probably the best way to protect yourself is to burn discs of all your critical material and to keep these discs somewhere other than the location of your computer, or probably even away from the home office itself. There are online data storage services available that are probably quite safe.

The disc route can get clunky, and you might want to think about a portable hard drive on which you can store your material. The advantage here is that you can overwrite material more quickly when you go to update information than you can when you use the CD-RW disc approach. However, a portable hard drive can get some pretty rough treatment; while the data may not be disturbed if yours gets dropped, you may never be able to access it because of mechanical failure. The little driveless memory sticks are ideal for transferring data and for short-term storage, although there seems to be some debate about how long the data can remain viable. CDs seem to be far more durable, and they are so inexpensive that in my opinion, this seems to be the way to go.

What to Do with All the Stuff You Can't Put on Your Computer

It would be nice if you could save all your records electronically; all you'd probably need would be a few discs that would take up no space at all. Unfortunately, there will be a lot of data coming your way that must be saved and cannot be put on a computer easily.

You could scan all the manuals that come with your equipment and save them as PDF files. You could even scan all of your receipts, legal documents, utility bills, and so on, but you wouldn't have much time left to do the things that make money. So, as onerous as it may seem, you still have to set up a system for storing these and many other documents that you will acquire as the owner of a home-based business. A hybrid system using both your computer and some file cabinets has to be somewhere in your plans.

Whether it gets saved to a disc or filed in a drawer will be up to you, and the decision will probably be determined by the way the data arrives to you. What you receive online will be saved electronically. What arrives in an envelope will probably be saved in a filing cabinet.

Roberta Roesch, who has written many articles and books on keeping business records organized, offered some advice.

I asked Roberta how someone who might be accustomed to working for a large firm that is already well organized should face the task of setting up a home office filing system. Her reply: "It's critical for someone running a small home business to have a calendar specifically devoted to the things that will occur regularly and pre-dictably. Leave space to include events that have to be marked as you go along, but the basic calendar should include such items as pay schedules, tax payment dates, equipment maintenance schedules—anything and everything that has a date critical to the running of your business should be on it."

Even well-planned and carefully documented calendars aren't perfect, and Roberta has a suggestion for that. "If you keep a paper calendar, get a set of different-colored magic markers and devote a color to each different event. Highlight taxes in red," she says with a wry smile. "If you keep your calendar electronically, simply use the range of colors available on your word processing program." For those who really like to play it safe, she suggests using both an electronic-based calendar and a paper calendar. "After you get it set up with all the different recurring dates and color cod-ing, just print it out and use both." She acknowledges that this has its problems. "If you keep two records of the same events, you must be sure that each jibes with the other. It's added work, but not too much work if safety is the issue for you," she said.

A calendar is just the beginning; equally as important is the system you use to file the paperwork you need to save. Roberta advises that you file alphabetically by cat-egory, or by date, and continues, "I'd suggest that consultants who work from a home office are probably better off if they file chronologically by category. However, this is a very subjective area; it's probably best to start this way and then shift to another arrangement if the system doesn't seem to be what you need."

Roberta explains that a system based on the frequency of use makes a lot of sense for the typical at-home business operation. "Setting up a file for items that must be retained for long period of time, but is referred to infrequently, is a good way to deal with such things as insurance policies, rental and lease agreements, bank records, and license and permit renewals. Another file for more frequently used files, such as correspondence, payroll records, supplier records, and invoice and payment records makes good sense."

All of this, of course, begs the question: How long should records be kept? Given that many of your records can be kept electronically, why not keep everything forever? After all, you never know when you might need some data, regardless of whether it is mandatory to retain the records. For example, if you were doing some long-range financial planning and you wanted some of your financial data that is past the expiration date set by the Fed, you'd be out of luck if you erased it. If you are keeping your records on paper, stick to the regulation dates as a minimum, but if you have the space to spare, hang on to them until you are absolutely sure that you will never need them again.

Record Retention

Here are some general guidelines for record retention:

Keep your canceled checks, receipts, and all other documents that might be needed to document a claim for at least as long as the statute of limitation requires for each item. Your accountant can fill you in on these dates.

You should keep all documentation of your federal tax returns for three years from the date the tax return was filed, or two years from the date the tax was actually paid, whichever is longer.

Some records should be kept forever, or at least until they are no longer valid. These include most of your corporate records, property records, and all insurance documents. If you employ others in the operation of your business, you are currently required to hang on to all employment tax records for at least four years.

For all other records, and there will be plenty of them, the decision should be made based on what the law requires and what would be the most difficult to replace if you needed them and couldn't lay your hands on them.

Until fairly recently, most decisions to save or chuck were made when you began tripping over the storage boxes on the way to your desk. Now that it is possible to store most of your sensitive data on a simple compact disc, it just makes sense to do what you can that way and never to chuck anything. Whether you put one or five gigabytes of data on a disc is immaterial. The physical size of the disc is the same. And, if you are like some others, including me, I have a dupe of every disc stored at a different location.

A Parting Shot

Ask the average home businessperson—whether a caterer, a manufacturer's rep, or a freelance writer—what bugs them most about their business, and they will all tell you the same thing: paperwork. Managing paperwork is the subject of hundreds of books. Books on accounting recordkeeping are done as a series, and could very well by sold by the yard or by the pound. So, if something that is close to your heart has been omitted here, please understand why. And, to keep you smiling as we move on to another topic, here's what some people you might recognize have said about (ugh) paperwork.

Julia Louis-Dreyfus

She, of the now-syndicated and still-popular TV show, *Seinfeld*, said, "I've actually considered going with my married name, Julia Hall, but all the paperwork . . ."

Frank Zappa

Guitarist, composer, film director, you name it, Zappa said, "It isn't necessary to imagine the world ending in fire or ice. There are two other possibilities: one is paperwork and the other is nostalgia."

Pearl Bailey

The multitalented Bailey nailed it with this statement: "The sweetest joy, the wildest woe is love. What the world needs is more love and less paperwork."

Wernher von Braun

One wonders whether we might have gotten to the moon sooner from Dr. von Braun's comment: "We can lick gravity, but sometimes the paperwork is overwhelming."

C. Northcote Parkinson

You have met this insightful man in earlier chapters, and here he continues to be as witty and relevant as you might expect: "The man whose life is devoted to paperwork has lost the initiative. He is dealing with things that are brought to his notice, having ceased to notice things for himself."

Peter De Vries

He, too, sees paperwork as anathema: "I love being a writer. I just can't stand the paperwork."

Frequently Asked Questions

1. *What effect do the home office deductions have on the taxes that must be paid when the house with a home office is sold?*
   In some cases, taxes will be levied that could reduce the real value of the deductions taken. However, you may be willing to put up with this, especially when every nickel counts in the start-up phase. This is a complex issue and not easily answered in a few sentences. Just make a note somewhere to check with your accountant when you plan to sell your house. Some accountants claim that, based on the deductions taken and the downstream consequences, it could be better to forgo some of the deductions that are available to you. Get a professional opinion before you do anything!

2. *What are the chances that I will face a federal audit?*
   Actually, they are pretty remote, unless you begin earning a lot of money rather quickly. The IRS has a number of red-flag issues that will trigger an audit, but it usually takes one dramatic event, or a combination of different red-flag events, before the alarm is sounded. In general, the more you make, the more likely you are to be audited. Most other audits are done randomly.

3. *Is there anything available from the IRS to help me get started?*
   The IRS has a number of very helpful reports and guides, available at www.irs.gov/businesses/small.

10 Protecting Your Home-Based Business

As with taxes, insurance and bonding are more of those pesky business details that you can't avoid. Regardless of your business type or size, you absolutely need insurance. What you might not need, however, are the extras that insurance salespeople sometimes to load you up with.

Many business owners find insurance to be complicated, but its importance can not be minimized. After all, by now you've probably invested considerable resources in time, money, and effort into your business. You'll count on your business to provide income and security for you and your family. It's a big deal, and you've got to protect it. The Independent Insurance Agents of America (IIAA) tell us that more than half of all home-based businesses in America are underinsured, mainly because business owners believe their businesses are covered by their homeowners policies.

The mistake, according to the IIAA, is that the typical homeowners policy provides only $2,500 for on-premise damage, and just $250 off premise. As you can imagine, those figures won't go far in the event of a claim.

Nobody really likes to deal with insurance (except for the people who sell it). It's expensive, and, every time you make a payment on it, you hope you never have to actually use it! Let's just take a quick look at the basics of insurance and how it works.

Sharing the Risk

Insurance is a means of sharing various types of risk with a large group of people. It's meant to protect you in the event that something goes wrong with your health or the health of a family member or your business or your home—the things in your life that are most important to you. If you get sick or are in an accident, you'll be in big trouble if you don't have insurance to cover lost income. If your house burns down, taking your business along with it, you're in really big trouble if you don't have insurance to cover the loss. We all hope to never need the insurances we buy, but nothing is for certain in life. So, we pool our money with lots of other people who also are hoping to not need the insurance, and we share the risk for when something goes wrong.

The insurance industry in the United States employs more than two million people in tens of thousands of companies. Insurers have the ability to get us out of big trouble, but also the ability to make our lives miserable with disputed claims, changing regulations, increased restrictions, and so forth. The insurance industry has a powerful lobby that puts a lot of pressure on the government agencies that are supposed to regulate it, and has been in the center of some very interesting legal and financial battles. When it comes right down to it, though, insurance is important because we need to have it. Let's take a look at some of the insurances that a home-based business owner must consider—both for himself or herself, and for the business.

Health Insurance

No matter how young or healthy you are, don't put yourself in a situation in which you are not covered by health insurance. As you know, the health care situation in this country is the topic of huge debate and discussion. Rallies are being held in Washington, D.C. to protest inequities in health care, politicians are trying to figure out how to slash the unsustainable costs of the system, and millions are Americans are left out in the cold without it.

If you have to pay for your own health care, it can be expensive. Still, just one illness or accident can prove to be catastrophic if you don't have it. If you've left a job where you had coverage to start your own business, you may qualify to extend your coverage with COBRA (Consolidated Omnibus Budget Reconciliation Act of 1985).

You Get What You Pay For

While it might be tempting to go for the lowest cost insurance you can find, remember that, often, you get what you pay for, or don't get what you don't pay for. Be sure to consider all the variables, including, but not limited to cost, when you're deciding what insurance to purchase.

This act requires your former employer to continue your coverage for up to 18 months after you leave the company, although you become responsible for paying for it. This can be pricey, but it's better than being uninsured. Meanwhile, you can be shopping around for the best policy you can find.

Disability Insurance

This is an insurance that nobody likes to think about, but, considering the fact that you have a greater chance of being disabled by the time you're 65 than dying, it's worth some consideration. Disability insurance protects you in the event that you become sick or are injured and are unable to produce an income. This insurance will provide an income until you're able to get back at it.

You can get either short term or long term disability insurance. Short term normally covers you for three to six months, while long term kicks in after six months. Since most business owners can't afford to be without a paycheck for an extended length of time (or any length of time, for that matter!) disability insurance is desirable.

When considering buying this type of insurance, think about, in the event that you were injured or become sick, how long you could go without income. This is called the elimination period, and, the longer you can delay starting the insurance, the better rate you'll get. This means, of course, that you'd have to have a rainy day fund available to support you and any dependents until the disability insurance was activated. Think about how long you'd be able to do that before selecting an elimination period option.

Also, take care to note how your policy defines "disabled." Some policies won't pay up unless you're actually in the hospital, and, you know how notoriously short hospital stays have gotten—even in the event of serious illness.

Life Insurance

Life insurance is even more of a downer to consider than disability, but necessary if you have a family. If you're young and single, you might be able to get away without life insurance, although a minimal policy that at least covers the cost of a funeral and burial is recommended.

The amount of life insurance you need depends on your age and circumstances. Most experts recommend that you have insurance worth between five and eight times the amount of your annual income. There are two types of life insurance, term and cash-value. Term life insurance, which you get when you pay a certain amount of money each year, is the more common of the two, and normally is less expensive than cash-value.

Comprehensive General Liability Insurance

Comprehensive general liability insurance is a biggie, because it helps to protect you in the event that you are sued. Even in a home-based business, chances are that, at some point, you'll meet with clients there, or they will come to pick something up or drop off something that you need. And, of course, there's always the possibility that someone will slip on an icy patch, or trip over your kid's skateboard, or look at your dog the wrong way and get bitten. Liability insurance also protects you in the event that someone is injured by you, or a member of your family, someone else's property is damaged or destroyed by you or a member of your family, and if someone claims you've slandered him.

Depending on the type of business you have and the potential risks involved, you may also have to consider coverages for professional liability, errors and omissions, liquor liability, off-premises liability, or product/completed operations coverage.

Business Property Insurance

If machinery or other property is damaged by fire or other disaster, business property insurance will cover the costs. Don't assume that your business property is covered by your homeowners insurance.

Business Interruption Insurance

Business interruption insurance applies in the event that your business is halted by a flood, hurricane, or other natural disaster or uncontrollable event. If a tornado blows through and badly damages your business, this insurance will cover your continuing operating expenses, such as the electric or phone bill, until you're up and running again, as well as income lost. It applies to situations such as a nearby wildfire, a fire at a neighboring structure that affects you, extended loss of electricity, and so forth.

Workers' Compensation Insurance

Workers' compensation is required for businesses in all 50 states, in some cases even if you're the only employee. If you are the only employee of a sole proprietorship, you can ask to have this requirement waived, but, in some cases, you will be required to buy this insurance. If you have employees, you must cover them with workers' compensation insurance.

How to Buy the Insurance You Need

There are several choices when buying insurance for your business, and, hopefully, you have an insurance agent who will recommend what makes the most sense for you. In some instances, you can get an endorsement on your homeowners policy that increases coverages to include your business. This typically is recommended only for very small businesses with low annual incomes ($5,000 or less), and it still may not be enough to cover all losses, so be sure you understand all the implications of endorsements before you add one.

There is something new available to home-based business owners called an in-home business policy. This limited package deal includes coverage to your business property and general liability coverage. It would cover you for lost income and ongoing business expenses in the event that your business had to shut because your house was damaged by fire or another cause. And, it contains limited coverage for loss of accounts receivable, valuable documents, and business property that is kept at a location other than your home.

Home-based businesses that operate in more than one location or manufacture products in a location other than the home might want to consider purchasing a business owner's package, known as a BOP. The coverages in this type of policy are broader than those of an in-home policy, and it can cover businesses with gross sales of up to $3 million.

The BOP is a packaged product, that is, a bundling of coverages. It's approved for use in 39 states, and is considered to be a good value for many types of businesses.

You can, and should, do your homework regarding the types of insurance you need for your home-based business and how it best makes sense to buy it. If you want to, you can buy business insurance online and hope you have the coverages you need, and, if something happens, you'll be able to get your claims processed to your satisfaction. If you prefer to work with a person, however, you'll want to rely on a dependable insurance agent to help you along.

Finding a Reliable Insurance Agent

Just as when you're looking for a banker, lawyer, or accountant, a good method of finding a reliable insurance agent is to talk to other entrepreneurs. You often get better rates if you buy more than one policy from the same agent, for instance, your auto and your homeowners insurance, instead of just your auto insurance—something you should keep in mind once you've found an agent you want to work with. Consider these other tips when looking for an insurance agent.

- Look for an agent with a professional designation. Chartered Property Casualty Underwriter (CPCU) is a coveted designation for agents who sell business insurance. Following the CPCU is the Certified Insurance Counselor (CIC). Both of these designations require ongoing training.
- Ask about the agent's employment history and find out how long he's been in the business.
- Find out what professional organizations he belongs to.
- Ask him to give you the names of a couple of clients with whom you can check for referrals.
- Make sure he's straightforward and willing to explain in detail about various policies and other insurance-related topics.
- Consider whether he seems interested in you and your business, or only in selling you insurance.
- Make sure he's familiar with the type of business you own and knows the ins and out of the particular needs of a home-based business.

Once you've found an agent you like, work to establish and maintain a relationship that's satisfactory to both of you. If your agent does not respond in a reasonable time to your phone call or e-mail, don't be afraid to say something about it. Insurance is an important aspect of your business, and you need someone you can rely on.

Watch Out!

Some insurance representatives will try to make you think you need all kinds of extra riders and policies that actually aren't necessary. You'll spend enough money on insurance without getting talked into buying extras that you don't need. There are many insurances that you do need, but some that you don't, so don't be talked into buying more than you need.

Frequently Asked Questions

1. *I am a 26-year-old male who just started his own business. I'm not married, although I plan to get married next year. I'm thinking it's going to be a stretch for me to pay for health care insurance, but I'm pretty healthy and I'm thinking maybe I can get by without it. What do you think?*

   Not having health care insurance at any age or under any circumstances is risky, but not having health insurance when you own your own business is particularly troublesome because it could put your business at risk. Shop around, and see what you can find. You probably can find some reasonably priced coverage if you go with higher deductibles and co-pays. At the very least, however, you should be covered in the event of a catastrophic illness or accident, which can happen any time to anyone.

2. *How do I go about finding an insurance agent I can trust?*

   The same way you would look for a lawyer, accountant, or other professional. Ask around for referrals, especially seeking out the advice of others in the same field that you're in. Check online, where you often can find ratings for professionals.

Marketing Your Company

While this chapter deals with marketing and how you'll go about planning to market your goods and services, it's necessary to first talk a little bit about sales. Sales and marketing both are designed to get customers to buy your products or services. And, while they're related, they're also very different.

Sales, actually, is the second step in the two-step process of sales and marketing. Marketing, which makes people aware of your goods or services, occurs before sales. Of course, you continue marketing your product after it has begun to sell, but in the two-step process, marketing is the first step. Sales is the actual process of convincing potential customers to buy your product or service.

Marketing, on the other hand, is the method or methods you use to make people aware of your product or service. After all, you can make the best mousetrap ever, but if nobody knows about it, the mice won't care at all.

Marketing entails advertising and promotional work. You need to come up with a plan determining the best way to let people know about your business and your product, and figure out how to execute that plan.

John Sortino, the entrepreneur who you met in chapter 1 and who has been mentioned in other chapters of this book, is known as something of a marketing guru. He was named in *Advertising Age* magazine as "One of America's Top 100 Marketing Stars" while leading the Vermont Teddy Bear Company. While CEO of that company, Sortino came up with the idea to have well-known New York City radio personalities market the bears during their live shows. Soon, Don Imus, Joan Hamburg, Howard Stern, and others were talking about Vermont Teddy Bears, telling listeners how cute and cuddly they were, and how they could order them just by calling an 800 number and talking to a "bear counselor" who would see them through the sale. The bears were customized to the exact specifications of the customer and mailed the next day in a specially decorated box, complete with breathing holes for the bear.

Customers loved these "Bear Grams," which came with add-ons such as Vermont maple syrup or locally made chocolates, and Sortino became well known for this marketing system. While he's moved on to other companies and other marketing strategies, he maintains a fondness for radio advertising.

Sortino said that while sales are key to establishing a successful business, you need to have a marketing plan in order to know how to sell your products and services. The marketing plan serves as a strategy for establishing and maintaining customer relationships. It sets the character, or culture of your company, and it spells out the avenues you'll use to move your company ahead, such as the Internet, TV, or your community's weekly shopper.

Company Culture

The company culture. Every organization, even if it's made up of just one person, has a company culture. It's the way you would like your prospects and clients to see you. It's the image you feel that would best position you to achieve your goals. Company culture is one of the areas that should be addressed in your marketing plan.

If you're starting out on your own, you'll need to decide the contents of your marketing plan. If you have partners or a board of directors, they should be involved in the writing of the plan so that everyone is on the same page as far as marketing.

Basically, your marketing plan defines who your market is, and how you're going to reach it. That's easy enough, right? To define your market, you first have to get to know it who it is.

Your market will depend largely on what type of business you have and the product or service that you're selling. If your product is wedding cakes, your market may be the people in your town and in surrounding towns. If you design computer software you could have an international market. Your market is whoever might buy your product or service. Once you've identified your market, you need to determine how to reach it.

Identifying Different Ways to Promote Your Company

If you get creative, you can probably come up with at least fifty ways of promoting your company. You could attend public gatherings and hand out pens with your company's name on them. You could buy billboards all over your county. You could do television infomercials, promote your company with a direct mail campaign, place ads in magazines or trade journals, announce special offers on Twitter and Facebook . . . the list goes on and on.

How you decided to market your company depends on who your market is. It would make no sense to run an ad in a trade journal for a product targeted to young moms, or on a rap station for a product targeted at senior citizens. A career consultant would advertise differently from someone selling jewelry, and a wedding planner differently than a computer repair person.

One rule that applies to nearly everyone, these days, is not to neglect Internet advertising. The Internet is simply too pervasive and widely used to ignore. Even if you only maintain a Web presence on your own web site, you've got to be online. Other means of advertising include the following:

- Newspapers and magazines
- Yellow Pages
- Signs and billboards
- Direct mail
- E-mail blasts
- Television
- Radio
- Trade shows
- Word of mouth
- Networking
- Public relations campaign

Patience is a Virtue

Don't expect instant results from your advertising, regardless of what method you choose. Consumers usually need to see or hear an ad several times before it starts to sink in. Be prepared to be patient.

Let's have a look at some of these marketing and advertising methods and what's good and not so good about them. As you consider each one, try to think about how it might apply to your particular business.

- The Internet. Some people love Internet advertising, while others swear it doesn't work. One thing is for sure, if you spend a lot of time on the Internet, you know how prevalent advertising is, and probably have a good idea of how annoying it can be. Online advertising comes in the form of contextual ads on search engine results pages, banner ads, Rich Media ads, social network advertising, online classified advertising, advertising networks and e-mail marketing, including e-mail spam. If you're interested in going the Internet route, you'll need to do some research to find out what type of advertising makes the most sense for your business. Some advantages of Internet advertising are that your ads can be targeted to particular audiences, it can be less expensive than traditional advertising, it's easy to track how many people are looking at your ads and responding to them either by buying something or redirecting to your web site, and you can reach a lot of people. Critics of Internet advertising say it can become an annoyance and turn off potential customers, ads often get lost in the clutter of some Internet pages, and much of it can be wiped out by ad blocking software. One thing for certain is that the Internet is here to stay, and advertising on it is too huge of a business to go away. Most experts advise that if you go with Internet advertising, it should be a piece of your marketing plan, and not the only type of advertising you do.

- Newspapers and Magazines. Newspaper and magazine advertising can be effective in reaching certain audiences, but it also can be expensive. Generally, the larger the publication's circulation is, the more expensive its ad rates will be. Be sure that the people reading the paper in which you place your ad are the people you want to reach. You can do that by checking out the publication's target audience and looking at the ads that your competitors are using. If you keep seeing an ad that's run over and over, you can figure it's paying off for the company running it. And, be sure you pay attention to the day of the week on which the ad runs. Newspapers, especially, cater to different audiences on different days with special sections, such as business, food, or entertainment. Although the future of newspapers is uncertain, many communities still have more than one publication, often a larger paper supplemented by smaller, more community-based papers and those geared mostly toward classified ads. If their audiences match yours, you can probably find some reasonable advertising rates. These days, don't be afraid to ask for a rate adjustment. Many newspapers are struggling and might be willing to offer you a discounted price.

- The Yellow Pages. Nearly every business belongs in the yellow pages because, even with all the Internet search engines available, the phone book is still the first place many people look when choosing a place from which to buy a product or obtain a service. Think about the last time you were out of town for a business trip or vacation. Especially if you were without a computer, you probably relied on the Yellow Pages to find a drug store, restaurant, nearby grocery store, or somebody who could repair your car. People use the Yellow Pages all the time. There used to be only one set of Yellow Pages, but the field has expanded an you may have to consider buying listings in more than one directory.

- Signs and Billboards. Signs located at your business tell people who you are and what you do. A sign can be especially important to a home-based business, although some entrepreneurs are reluctant to call attention to their home businesses, for a variety of reasons. Signs and billboards in locations other than at your business can help to direct people to you.

- Direct Mail. A direct mail campaign can let existing customers know about changes and improvements you've made to your business, and is a great method of staying in touch. If you know how to employ the mail merge features on your office computer, you probably can do a direct mailing to existing customers without too much trouble, since you already have their contact information. You also can buy lists of potential customers who you want to notify about your business. You get them from a mail list broker, and you can find these firms online or by consulting the Yellow Pages of your phone book. Make sure that you request very targeted lists, so you can find the people you want to reach. Just be sure that your mailing is attractive and interesting looking so it doesn't end up, unread, in the trash can.

- E-mail Blast. A sort of electronic direct mail, you can e-mail a list of clients or potential clients about your business and what's going on with it. If you do this too often, however, you will risk annoying the recipient and perhaps being added to their SPAM list so that your emails are diverted away from their inboxes.

- Television. Television advertising used to be prohibitively expensive for small businesses, and, in some cases, it still is. The great surge in the number of cable stations, however, means that often TV can be a doable advertising option. Cable stations have pretty well defined audiences, so you can target your ads to those you want to reach. Local news programs are popular in many areas, and can provide opportunities for reaching potential customers, since you can count on the fact that local people are watching them. TV stations have advertising sales representatives who will meet with you. Be sure you ask about the station's Nielsen ratings, which indicate how many viewers the channel has.

- Radio. Some people think of radio as being sort of an old-fashioned form of advertising, but lots of people still use it, so it must be reasonably effective. Radio's strength is that it lets you target a select market, because different radio shows are geared toward different audiences. Listen sometime to the variety of businesses that advertise on the radio, and on what types of shows the ads are run. If you decided to advertise on the radio, keep in mind that most people listen when they're in their cars. Drive times are prime times for radio advertising.

- Trade Shows. Trade shows have value because they attract people who already are interested in your product or service. Someone doesn't come to a jewelry show, for instance, if she's not interested in jewelry, and probably in buying jewelry. Trade shows are great places to introduce new products, and, if you plan in advance, you can offer a special event, such as press conference or cocktail reception, to draw people to your booth.

- Word of Mouth. This is the one kind of advertising that works for everybody, and it's arguably the most valuable kind. Positive referrals from existing customers to prospective customers are the most sure-fire way to bring in new business, although you have to be patient, as it can be a slow process. Remember that there's nothing wrong with asking happy customers and clients to please refer you to their friends and colleagues. When you've treated customers well and delivered the product or service you promised, they usually are happy to help you spread the word.

- Networking. Some people are natural-born networkers, and they often have a real advantage over people who find it difficult to chat about their businesses, trade information, and conduct the many other aspects of business that accompany networking. Good opportunities for networking are available by joining your local chamber of commerce; a young professionals' group; or volunteering to help with a community project, such as a capital campaign for a local library or boys and girls club. Being known in your community is a great asset for an entrepreneur, and putting yourself out there so you get to know others and others know you doesn't have to cost much at all. All in all, networking is a great and inexpensive means of marketing that shouldn't be overlooked.

Public Relations Campaigns

It's important to understand the distinction between advertising and public relations, although the two are related. Advertising generally is when you pay someone to put your company's name someplace that it will be seen or heard by others. This can range from paying for a radio ad to hiring a plane to fly along edge of the ocean with a banner advertising your business.

Public relations is more of an effort to publicize your company in different ways, such as pitching a story about it to the business department of your local newspaper or an area business journal or sending out press releases announcing new products, employees, or services. Businesses sometimes use clever methods of getting publicity for themselves without having to pay for it. A story appeared recently in a mid-sized city paper featuring the employees of a regional real estate firm. During the week before the Fourth of July, employees of the firm's eleven offices throughout a four-county area would be planting American flags on the lawns of all the properties listed with the agency, the story read. A representative of the real estate firm was quoted as saying the move was in celebration of the great ideals of America and as a wish for a quick economic recovery for the country. The paper even included a photo of employees and their flags, ready to begin distribution.

This sort of publicity often is perceived as being more valuable, and more credible than paid advertising, and can provide a great advantage for a company. Be creative in thinking about what your business is doing that might set it apart from other businesses. If you're just getting off the ground, try contacting the business department of your local paper to see if it might send a reporter out to do a story on you. Learn how to write a good press release so you can promote your business. You can find all kinds of press release samples online.

Just be sure, however, to not make a pest of yourself by overly promoting or bugging your local media representatives. Reporters and editors have been known to ignore press releases when the sender is overbearing or too annoying.

Establishing a Marketing Budget

So, now that we know a little about the various forms of marketing and advertising, let's talk about how much you should think about spending on marketing.

There are a lot of variables when it comes to figuring out a marketing budget. Some companies simply are able to afford more advertising than others. Some types of businesses require greater marketing efforts than others. One thing is for sure, advertising and other marketing costs can add up quickly, so you need to figure how much you're able to spend, and how to get the best value for your money.

The best way to begin establishing a marketing budget is to get an idea of the costs of different types of advertising. You can find most of that information online or by making a couple of phone calls. Add up some of the prices and you'll get an idea of what you'd get and how much it would cost. Don't make the mistake of committing to advertising that you're not sure you'll be able to afford.

The advertising industry recommends that a small business spend between five and seven percent of its gross sales, but that doesn't mean that should be the goal of every small business. When it comes right down to it, you should spend an amount that you're comfortable with. Most starting businesses don't have a lot of extra money for marketing, and that's fine. Start small, look for marketing methods that don't cost very much, and do what you can. You can always increase your spending later on.

Getting Some Help with Your Marketing Plan

There's no shortage of marketing services, so if you're interested in getting some help, you'll be sure to be able to find some. There are market researchers, market analysis firms, and marketing consultants. There also are public relations firms, graphic designers, Web designers, print shops, creative services, and so on and so forth.

So, how do you know, first, if you should consider hiring someone to help you with your marketing efforts, and, second, who that person or company should be? If you decide to hire someone, how much should you be prepared to spend?

Chances are that you can do most of your marketing work yourself, or with the help of a sales representative from your local paper or cable TV station or wherever you decide to advertise. Once you begin advertising, you'll be assigned an account representative who will help you plan your budget and give you ideas. If you plan to do print advertising in a magazine, newspaper, or other publication, you may need to hire someone to create an ad for you. But don't assume this is true until you check, because newspapers and magazines often have people on staff who will create your ad as part of the cost of advertising. If you're interested in television advertising, talk to the sales representative at the TV station. He or she might be able to help you create an ad, or at least answer your questions.

If you want to do a direct mailing, you might have to talk to somebody about renting a mailing list. If you decide for whatever reason to do a more comprehensive marketing campaign, you might have to hire a marketing person or a firm to direct it. Often, though, marketing efforts are best handled by those who know the company best—you, or you and your partners.

If you do find that you need help with any aspect of your marketing efforts, think about who you know. Perhaps you've heard of a former newspaper reporter who's opened her own public relations firm, or someone who's left an agency to start his own graphic design firm. Maybe you know someone who works for a big marketing firm but does freelance work on the side. Do you know anybody who works for your area's newspaper who might be able to offer some advice on how you can submit a press release or request a story about your business? Or an advertising representative at the local radio or TV station? Even if you want your advertising to extend beyond your own area, people who work in the field locally should be able to tell you how to proceed and what questions you need to ask.

Generally, if you're trying to determine who your market is, you'd use market researchers, a market analysis firms, or a marketing consultant. If you want help in conveying an image of your company, or getting publicity for it, you'd probably want to try a marketing consultant or public relations firm. For help with creating ads, signs, brochures, or promotional pieces, look to graphic designers, print shops, or creative services firms.

If you decide to hire an individual or firm to help you with your marketing efforts, understand that their costs will vary greatly, depending on who you approach. Top-rate consultants might charge a couple of hundred dollars an hour, while a freelance graphics designer may work for $40 an hour. Here are a couple of tips to keep in mind:

- If you use an ad or marketing agency, there are different levels of employees, some of whom charge more than others. Be sure you know who you're paying for what jobs.
- If you're going to be charged an hourly fee, ask for an estimate of how much time will be involved. You might want to limit the number of hours to be spent on a particular project, or set a price that's not to be exceeded.
- Negotiate. You might not have much leverage with a one-time job, but if you're planning on throwing more work at the person or firm you've hired in the future, you might be able to work some kind of deal. Don't be afraid to ask.
- Set a budget for marketing costs, and make sure to work within it. It's frightening how fast advertising and marketing costs can mount.

Your marketing plan, like your business plan, is a tool. It should be used to build your business in an orderly way. It should keep you focused on certain attainable goals, and it should be flexible enough to help you navigate unanticipated roadblocks, as well as to take advantage of positive conditions you didn't foresee when you wrote it.

A good marketing plan is based on a clear understanding of who and what your target market is, and should help you toward a better understanding of who and what your business is, as well.

Frequently Asked Questions

1. *Just how flexible can a marketing plan be? Are there any rules that can be applied when changes seem necessary?*
    Your marketing plan isn't set in stone, and it will change as your business grows and changes. Keep in mind, however, that changes shouldn't be made just for the sake of making changes, but should be made when it's apparent that major opportunities or major problems are on the horizon, or if it looks like the focus of your business is shifting.

2. *I'm tempted to put all of my advertising dollars into cable television. It makes sense to me because I watch a lot of cable TV and notice the ads I see.*
    It's rarely a good idea to put all of your advertising money into one market. You should consider all of the options available to you, decide how much you're willing and able to spend, and then spread the money out over a range of opportunities to maximize exposure and reach as many people as possible.

12 | Looking to the Future

Owning a business is sort of like having a child—you're always looking ahead for it and wondering what it will be like in another year, or five years, or ten. And, just as children don't always follow a predictable course, neither do businesses. We've seen a great many businesses fail in the recent past, due to the current economic conditions, but we've also seen a great many new ones started, as people who have lost their jobs or were anticipating losing their jobs rethought their futures and went the entrepreneurial route.

Hopefully, you're in a position where your business is expanding, and you're looking at some positive changes. You might be looking to hire some employees, or branch out into other products or services, or expand your business, or perhaps even to sell it and start again with something else.

If, after you've been operating your business for a while, you realize you're looking at some major changes, be assured that, although expanding a business or merging with another business presents challenges and raises uncertainty, it almost always is easier than starting a business from scratch, and you've already done that!

So, if you're looking at big changes for your business, and perhaps your life, understand that you're smarter, wiser, and more confident than you were the first time around. It's likely that you're a little more humble, too, so if you don't feel any more confident, that's probably why.

A home-based business is usually a labor of love—something you do mainly because you really like the work and you want to build something for yourself. Few do it because they envision selling it someday, but many do see their businesses outgrowing the home office. At the moment, however, you are probably still trying to put wheels on your wagon and haven't given much thought to what you might do with the business later. Your notion of expansion at the moment is probably limited to reaching the point where the business is in the black and you can cut back to a six-day week. However, as busy as you might be cranking the business up, you should at least have some idea of what you can do with a business down the road.

This chapter addresses the decisions you will face later—to maintain your original idea of working from a home office, expanding beyond the limitations of a home office, and finally, selling the business. How you see your later years now will help you plan in an orderly fashion, and will probably prevent you from making some serious mistakes. This isn't really a big deal, especially since you probably have your hands full at the moment growing your business. But hang in there through these last pages; you won't regret it!

Hiring Employees

Employees are necessary to most businesses. If you've reached the point where you need to think about hiring, that means that either your business has grown and you need some help to handle the extra work, or you're making a concerted effort to grow the business with the help of an extra person or people. Either way, it's a good thing!

Before you can put out the word that you're looking for help, however, you'll need to have your ducks in a row. Employees can help you to bring your business to a new level, but they also will change the tenor and tone of your business, simply by their presence. If you're used to running your business single-handedly, bringing in even one employee will be a change for you. Of course, you might very well enjoy having some company and someone with whom to share the work load. In preparation for hiring, keep in mind the following considerations:

- You'll need to get an employer federal ID number.
- Be sure to be aware of how to conduct an interview; there are legalities involved.
- You'll need to find out how much an employee of the type you'll be hiring will expect to be paid.
- Will you be offering benefits to an employee or employees?
- Regulations and policies for employees should be established.
- Your employee may need a desk, phone, computer, and other supplies.
- How will you advertise for an employee?

- What will be the specific responsibilities or your employee or employees?
- You'll be responsible for Social Security, Medicare, workers' compensation, and unemployment taxes.
- How will you go about training your employee or employees?

After you've taken some time to think about all those things, consider the fact that hiring employees during a recession brings with it some advantages. There are a lot of people out of work and looking for jobs, so you should have no shortage of applicants, and there are likely to be some very qualified ones. Keep in mind that the recession will end eventually and jobs will become more plentiful. This means that, if you find a qualified person to hire now and would like to keep him or her on board for the long haul, don't try to skimp on what you pay because you know that the person needs the job. Pay your employee what he or she is worth and work to establish a lasting relationship.

You can look for employees by word of mouth, through a classified ad, online job boards or social networking sites like Craigslist, or through an employment agency. In the current economic condition, you shouldn't have trouble attracting applicants. It's necessary, however, to know how to screen and interview potential employees so you end up getting someone who will benefit your business.

If you're not looking to hire a full-time employee, you might think about hiring for part-time or, depending on your business, bringing on a contractor or freelance person to help you. If you're a graphic designer with an at-home business, for instance, you may encounter periods during which you have more work than you can handle, but there are other times when business is slow. Finding a freelance designer to work with you during the busy times would make more sense than hiring someone and either having to let him go, or having him be nonproductive during the slow times.

Growing a Home-Based Business

A home-based business is personal. Having such a business means that your work life and your home life intersect, usually with one becoming part of the other. You might make it a point to take a little time to talk to your neighbor every day, or to have lunch with your wife when she's not at work. You might wait for your kids to get home from school and chat with them for a few minutes about their days. Pretty much, your business and the rest of your life overlap, and hopefully, you've figured out the balancing act necessary to make that situation work.

And, it's likely that you're still running the business pretty much on your own, and the business is pretty much yours alone. Sure, you might have some part-time help, and maybe even have set up some appropriate strategic alliances with other business people. But it's you that your customers think of when they call to schedule a service or place an order.

Take a sick day, go on vacation, or just don't reply to a customer's call for a few days, and you will soon see just how critical you are to your business.

The first few years of running a home-based business is a shakedown cruise of your business ship. You'll find some leaks in the hull that need to be repaired. The engines will be balky until they are properly run in. And topside will take a pounding from anxious clients and aggressive competitors. But, by the time you realize that your ship is seaworthy, you will be on a good course and focused mainly on getting enough work or sales to meet your projections, plus a bit more so that you're able to truthfully report that you are growing. And, all the while, you're looking for and hoping for more work, more clients, more sales, and more growth. You're looking for your business to be truly successful.

Whether you are running your home-based business part-time or are working at it full-time, there will come a point when you have to decide what to do with the business. If it just isn't making it, regardless of what you do to promote it, you may have to close down and possibly try again later. And, remember what you read way back in chapter 1, that failing at a business doesn't make you a failure by any means.

Hopefully, though, the issue you'll be looking at is not that your business hasn't taken off, but that it's caught on beyond your expectations. When that occurs, you face another set of issues.

If you're running and work at your business on a part-time basis, you will probably have to decide whether to continue part-time or expand to make it full-time. There are far too many business and personal issues to address here, but in general, a decision to go full-time should be made only after careful planning and research on the current state of your field and its growth potential for you. Nothing is foolproof, but with good planning, you will have a far better chance of succeeding than if you go at it blindly, just as you did when you first started your company from nothing

It's important to know just what you want to achieve with your business. Do you see it mainly as an adjunct to the income you get from full-time work, or do you see it turning into your full-time work? You may even be in that fortunate position of having a part-time business that's taken off to the point where you either have to make the move to full-time, or cut back on some of your business.

Expansion should be based on two things: a growing market for your product or services, and your ability to compete efficiently for a share of that business. A growing market can be seen from several perspectives. Overall growth in your field will raise all boats, including yours. However, even in a shrinking market, you may be able to prosper.

Rarely does any business collapse completely without warning. Rather, as a business sector contracts, many of your competitors will leave the field. If you can withstand the downturn and have the capability to get and keep the customers that others are abandoning, it's possible to actually grow when others fail. However, you have to be certain that the decline in your field is a cyclical phenomenon and that business will return on an uptick of the cycle. Home-based business often are better able to survive and possibly even prosper during downturns simply because of their low overhead. The obvious tip here is to avoid taking on the heavy overhead as some of your competitors might be doing.

For now, let's assume that your business isn't exactly growing by leaps and bounds, but that you're doing just fine. You've got some good and loyal customers, and you know that you probably could attract even more customers if you were to really make a concerted effort to do so. Only you can decide whether that's the way you want to go. Maybe you're perfectly content with your business at just the size it is, and you have no desire to grow it to be larger and more complicated. Whether you want to expand or remain small is a personal decision that only you can make. Remember that, the larger you get, the less you will do of the work that got you into your own business in the first place. If you really enjoy the hands-on work involved with a small business, running a larger business may not be for you. It's quite possible to be happy and content with a small business that you own and operate yourself in a hands-on manner. And, while you might happen to enjoy that approach, you may have friends who do the same work as you who have expanded dramatically and are just as happy running a larger firm. It's what makes them happy. There are no answers that fit everyone. You really have to get a handle on just who you are and what you want from life and take the appropriate path.

If you are at the point of deciding whether you think expanding your business might be the way to go, consider the following questions.

Why Should You Expand Your Business?

Perhaps there are great opportunities to be seized, and it seems like a logical time go expand. Or, maybe your business is your full-time livelihood, and you're feeling pressured to keep it growing. In either one of those cases, though, the real decision is just how much expansion will be possible if you plan to stay a small, home-based business, or if your goal is to ramp up to something a lot larger. Remember that a small business will usually remain fragile, no matter how successful you are, simply because *you* are the business. A larger business can be less fragile, but it can become a cash-eating machine if you are not careful. And, as mentioned earlier, it can force you to divert your attention from doing the work of the business to running the business.

Meet Marc Dorio, a home-based management consultant who specializes in management development and corporate human resource consulting. With more than twenty-five years' experience and graduate degrees in organizational psychology, Marc includes Fortune 500 and Fortune 100 companies on his client list. He is the author of *The Personnel Manager's Desk Book, The Staffing Problem Solver, The Complete Idiot's Guide to the Perfect Interview, The Complete Idiot's Guide to Getting the Job You Want,* and *The Complete Idiot's Guide to Career Advancement.* Marc teaches college courses, and appears frequently as a guest on national TV shows—all of this while working from a home office in historic western New Jersey, in clear view of the Delaware River. He summed up the issue of the manner in which the role in your business could change as your business expands quite succinctly.

"If you like the idea of supporting a payroll and managing a business more than doing the work of the business, then by all means go for the growth, " Marc said. "On the other hand, if you can satisfy your personal goals without taking on the responsibilities growth implies, then staying small is the way to go. Don't let friends and even relatives try to influence your decision. This is something you will work very hard at long after the decision has been made."

Marc does point out, however, that there is another alternative for the person who would like to grow a bigger business, but who really prefers to remain at the forefront of the client work being done. "Think about hiring support people to allow you to continue to do the work that gives you pleasure. A few good part-time people who handle all the details of your business while you continue to do the client work is a really good way to go."

Should You Expand Your Product or Service Base or Keep a Narrow Focus?

Perhaps your home-based business is still selling just the one or two products or services that you started out with. Maybe you're still baking and decorating wedding cakes, without having branched out into favors or candles of other wedding-related products. Or, maybe you're still offering a specialized consulting service directly to clients, or by subcontracting work from larger consulting firms. Growth depends on the need for the services you offer, the current competition, the cost of expansion, and the long-term potential for the services or products you offer. Here are a few questions you need to ask before you make any big decisions:

- Which of your present services or products are the most profitable?
- Is there a growing need for your number-one service or product?
- Can you sell more of your number-one service or products to your present client base, or will you have to grow by seeking new customers or clients?
- What related services or products can you sell to your present clients or customers?
- Is there a growing need for a service or product that you can provide that might eclipse the need for the services or products you currently sell?
- What will it cost to expand the services or products you offer to present clients, as well as to expand by seeking new clients?
- Will any of your expansion plans require outside help or expanded facilities—either an office or other facility outside your home, or an expansion of your present home office?
- What are the short- and long-term investment requirements for any expansion you might consider?

If you reach this point, it's time that you to pull out your business and marketing plans. Both should contain information that will inform your decisions and direct your way. Probably the most critical decisions you will have to make, as it seems to go in life, will involve money. You will need to know whether you can expand with existing capital, or whether you will have to borrow money to do it. If your business is part-time and you don't depend on the income for routine living expenses, you might be able to finance an expansion simply by plowing the income you're making from the business back into it. However, this can take a lot longer than if you were to invest directly, possibly with borrowed capital. Be sure you carefully assess all the personal and business risks before making any decisions.

How Big Can a Home-Based Business Get?

If it becomes necessary, you probably can easily locate part-time backup help such as bookkeepers, clerical staff, and even semiprofessional assistants who usually are readily available to either work right in your office, or as independent contractors from their own home offices. Help from this quarter will get you to the point where you can maximize the time you put into the business, whether it's a part-time shop or a full-time operation. However, what happens when you are overworked professionally?

You may have staff taking care of the details, but perhaps you are the person who performs the services or provides the products that your clients and customers pay for. This is where many small businesses are most vulnerable to making mistakes, or even plain bad decisions. Owners see potential for growth, but are unsure about the best way to go. It's at this point where you will be really tested about your commitment to remaining a small, home-based business.

Consider this, however, there is potential for turning a home-based business into a larger business that must operate from outside the home and focus on a system that has allowed many home-based business owners to build large and profitable practices while still operating from their home offices – an enviable trick. This is accomplished using what's called the strategic alliance.

Growing Your Business with Strategic Alliances

Basically, a strategic alliance is two or more people or organizations working together to achieve a common goal. This, however, is more than just a buzz phrase. It's more than two home-based business owners simply helping each other out on an as-needed basis. In a strategic alliance, the word *strategy* is the defining concept. A strategy is a long-term plan, and by forming strategic alliances, many entrepreneurs have leveraged their positions greatly, because each one counts on the other for something specific. In some cases, an alliance between two entrepreneurs involves filling in skill gaps; in others, it involves providing backup when one of you has an overload of work. In all cases, it requires a willingness to work closely together, even when you might also be competing in each other's areas. In short, it requires a rather high level of trust between or among the participants. Although there might appear to be a lot of room for mischief, very few entrepreneurs seem to have had bad experiences with these alliances. The more common complaint seems to be that one of the partners was unable to perform as "advertised." But, this is no reason to avoid considering a strategic alliance should the need arise. As with any sort of partnership, though, what is absolutely necessary before entering a strategic alliance, however, is a thorough understanding of one another's abilities and skills.

Surprisingly, one of the major reasons that people in certain fields cite for becoming involved in strategic alliances is not to ramp up billing, but to take advantage of growing international opportunities, and to fend off competitors. More than a few well-known entrepreneurs have greatly expanded their international reach by forming strategic alliances, and it's been a very productive way for many to gain a presence in smaller countries where the cost to operate their own branch might be prohibitive. This means that an expansion could occur by being the strategic partner of an offshore consulting firm seeking a presence in the United States.

Expanding Your Business in Other Ways

Business expansion, of course, can occur in other ways than through strategic alliances, and the expansions can be local, regional, national, or international. You can expand your business by buying another business, licensing a product or process, or outsourcing part of your business so you can concentrate on the aspects of it that you enjoy the most and do the best, thereby causing your business to grow. If you're of a mind to, you could take your company public, which means finding investors and selling of pieces of the company, or you might even consider franchising your business. Depending on what you've had going on, you could expand by adding a direct mail component, or selling goods or services on the Internet. There are many ways to expand a business, and what you decide to do depends on the business you've got, your aspirations for the future, the balance you've got between your business and personal lives, your financial situation, and other factors.

Regardless of what method you choose, expanding your business will require careful thought and planning. You'll need to redo your business plan, look at all the numbers, and make sure you understand completely and thoroughly where the business has been and where it appears to be heading. You'll need to figure out how much capital you'll need in order to expand your business, and where that money will come from. If you'll need investors, you'll have to start identifying possibilities and setting up some appointments. One of the first things to consider would be the scope of your planned expansion. Let's take a brief look at the implications of the types of expansions mentioned above: local, regional, national, and international.

Local Expansion

Your home-based catering business has taken off, and you need more space. Your home facility, even with the renovations you did and the extra kitchen equipment you bought, can no longer handle all the work you've taken on, and you're thinking of setting up shop somewhere near your home.

Local expansion the easiest way of expanding your business because it's convenient. You're right there to see what's going on. Plus, you've already got the name recognition, and you already know that people like your catering business. The advertising you do could be revised to include your new location without costing any more than you're already paying. Finding a new location might be a little stressful, but if you keep in mind factors such as taxes, parking, cost of leasing, security, availability, competition, population, growth patterns, traffic patterns, personal considerations, and so forth, you'll be fine. You'll need to decide whether your home office will move along with your facilities, or if you'll keep your office within your home and merely move your operations facility. With current real estate prices low in many areas, it's actually a great time to be looking for additional space.

Regional Expansion

As with local expansion, regional expansion is manageable because you're right there to keep an eye on things. You also can use some of the same advertising without running up extra costs. When you're known within a certain area, it makes it easier to expand regionally. Chances are that people within your region have already heard of your catering business, especially if you've been diligent about spreading the word. If you're thinking of expanding regionally, it's a good time to drum up some publicity in the form of public relations. You'll want to write—or find someone else to write—a press release announcing your expansion to send to area newspapers, regional magazines, and business journals. Be sure to include a listing of your services, how long you've been in operation, and some of the more memorable events that you've catered.

National Expansion

National expansion is a big deal, and probably beyond the scope of most readers at this time, but it might be fun to think about for your future. National expansion means you've got to somehow get the whole country to know about your product or services, and, that's not easy. However, with lots of capital and planning, it's possible.

Nearly all national businesses started out as regional ones—remember that. Papa John Schnatter of pizza fame started his business in a broom closet in Louisville, Kentucky, and, who hasn't heard of Papa John's? Bill Rosenberg was a member of a lower-middle class family when he scraped together some money to start a couple of donut shops—you've got it! Dunkin' Donuts.

National expansion, of course, isn't something that you'd enter into lightly or without plenty of market research and planning. What sells in New York City won't necessarily translate to Portland, Oregon, or Miami, where there are different people with different preferences and expectations. A product or service that's wildly popular in Las Vegas might fall flat in Philadelphia. Or, it might have much greater appeal to urban people than rural, or the other way around.

You'd also have to think about distribution, logistics of manufacturing, and many other factors. You've no doubt got the point that national expansion is complicated and, if you ever decide to go that route, will require a great deal of preparation and planning. Still, it's fun to consider, and who knows what lies in store for your business.

International Expansion

International expansion is difficult because every country has its own laws and regulations, and you've got to be sure you know what they are. If you're going to set up shop in a foreign country, you have to be willing to invest a great deal of time to learn all the regulations that apply, not to mention cultural considerations and other factors.

If you don't have international business experience yourself, you'll need to find someone who does to help you set up and run an international business. You'll also need a lawyer who's well versed on global business as well as a really good chief executive officer or chief financial officer who has significant international business experience. There also are the challenges of staffing international businesses and the logistical considerations of running a company from another country, assuming you'll also maintain domestic operations and continue living in the United States.

Still, while global expansion used to be pretty confined to major companies, technology is making it possible for some small companies to compete. A Web site can provide global presence and make it possible to conduct business without actually setting up a facility elsewhere. E-mail and other electronic forms of communication makes it as easy to be in touch with someone in Argentina as your neighbor down the street.

The Internet makes it possible to easily research foreign business regulations and other factors, and satellite systems that you can lease from vendors keep you hooked into your distributions channels.

It's a different world than even a decade ago, with the way we communicate and do business changing constantly. Global expansion, however, requires extensive research in order to develop business and marketing plans. You'd need to understand the tax structure of the country you'd expand into, the status of supplies, competing companies already established there, the country's system of currency, and other factors too numerous to list here. If you get to the point where you're seriously considering international expansion, you probably would do well to hire a consultant with extensive international experience to help guide you through the process.

If you're planning to expand your business through any capacity, whether it be a local expansion, through a strategic partnership, or you're going global, make sure you're expanding for the right reasons, and that you have the financial capacity you need to be successful.

Selling Your Business

While looking to expand your business is one possibility, there's also a chance that, at some time in the future, you'll be looking to sell it. If you're just getting started at this point, you might not even have the capacity to consider selling your business. Or, building your business and then selling it and starting another one might have been your plan all along. Some entrepreneurs move routinely from one business to the next, starting, building, and selling. Even if you can't imagine selling your business at this point, the time may come when you want to address that issue.

Many small businesses are sold because the owner wants to retire. He's started the business and built it up and it's doing fine, but he's ready to spend a few months every winter in Florida and put that fishing boat to good use. Another reason businesses are sold is because somebody comes along and makes you an offer that you can't refuse. Or, your personal circumstances could change, such as with an illness or divorce, forcing you to sell. Maybe you've just decided that owning your business is too much hassle and you're ready to be an employee again and let someone else worry about taxes and insurance and all the rest that goes along with being an entrepreneur. It's true that we've compared owning a business to raising a child. There's a big difference, however, in that under certain circumstances you can sell your business and move on with no guilt at all, something that would be impossible with a child!

Those are some reasons that people might consider selling their businesses. Now, let's take a look at why someone might consider buying your home-based business.

- You own a niche that other businesses have not been able to gain a foothold in.
- You are seen as a competitor who could be neutralized by a strategic acquisition.
- Your business is strong and has a good reputation and a buyer is convinced that he can continue to run it successfully.
- The type of business you're selling is at a strong point and the potential buyer is looking toward expansion opportunities.
- The prospective buyer thinks that buying an established business will be easier than starting a similar business from scratch.

Steps to the Successful Sale of Your Business

If you've decided to sell your home-based business, think about whether you want to sell the business yourself, or whether you might want a business broker to handle the sale and all necessary transactions. You will surely need to work with your accountant and your lawyer.

Typically, business brokers ask for a 10 percent commission on the sale price if it's a million dollars or less. Most have a descending commission scale as the purchase price gets larger. These rates vary from business to business, so it's a good idea to talk with several brokers before you make a choice. Keep in mind that while a smaller commission rate is always attractive, it's the skill and experience record of the broker that should be the key element in your decision.

Selling a business is not an easy task, even when you have a business broker working on your case. If you've reached the point where you want to retire or for

Business Sale Tip . . .

One of the first things a prospective buyer's accountant will do is check to see if you are up-to-date with your tax payments. If you are unable to make a current payment, file for an extension. Don't make it look like you're dodging a tax bullet.

some other reason you don't have the enthusiasm you had when you first started the business, don't let your guard down as you go through the sale process. Without proper attention, you just might leave too much on the table, and in your hurry to be off to the golf course or into another career you could very well commit yourself to details that you will regret later, or end up selling your business for less than what it's really worth.

Be Specific about Why You Want to Sell Your Business

People who buy businesses are usually very concerned about the "real" reason some-one wants to sell. "Why would someone want to sell a business that is this profit-able?" is a common question business brokers are asked. Even when the real reason is retirement, or looking to get into a different business, it seldom satisfies buyers who might be committing a significant amount of their own money to the acquisition. This means that you should not only be personally honest about your reasons, but also that you should be prepared to carefully document all the benefits and problems that will go with the acquisition. Your accountant should be able to document all the figures to a prospect's satisfaction, but you must be able to tell your story honestly and convincingly.

If your business has simply gotten to be too much work and you're not looking to take on partners or hire more employees or expand it by forming a strategic alliance or other means, be honest about it. Your view of what is too much work might not be daunting someone else. If you are having employee or alliance disputes, be honest about them. Apart from the importance of being truthful, if you don't reveal what's going on, you could be open to charges of falsification of information. If you are selling because you have not achieved the success or profit levels you envisioned, be honest about it. But be sure to detail exactly what you *have* done to get where you stand now. A prospective buyer may see that you are on the verge of better business, but you may just be worn out from trying.

Setting a Price for Your Business

If you decide to sell your business, be sure to get the advice you need about how to do it. There are different formulas for coming up with a sell price, and all sorts of ways to negotiate a business sale. You'll need to decide if you'd like to stay on board for a year as a consultant or officer. If you're starting another business, will you actually be competing against the one you're selling? What kind of financial arrangement will you have with the buyer? All these things, and many more, must be considered if you're going to sell, so, unless you happen to be an expert in business negotiations, depend on the business broker, if you have one, and your accountant and lawyer to help you.

Determining the Best Time to Sell Your Business

As with planning for growth, you should plan well ahead and carefully for the sale of your business—at least a year in advance is advised. There are different stages to selling a business, such as solidifying the operations, preparing a marketing prospectus about the company's financials and performance records, marketing to prospective buyers, working with prospective buyers as they investigate all aspects of your business, the actual sale of the business, and post sale business. So, you see, you can't decide to put your business up for sale and expect the process to begin and end within a few months. If you have the luxury of time and your business is cyclical and predictable, plan to look for buyers during the upside of the cycle.

Business Sale Tip . . .

Go over your tax returns for the past few years and see where it might be necessary to add back any discretionary expenses you might have made, such as a bumped-up salary in a particular year, and possibly even an automobile expense. A prospective buyer's accountant will want to know what the real costs of running the business are.

Sell It Yourself or Get Some Professional Help

If you decide to seek the services of a business broker, you'll go about finding one in much the same way you located your lawyer, accountant, and insurance agent. Ask friends and professional colleagues for their recommendations, and if no one can help, turn to the Yellow Pages listing of business brokers. If you have some to choose from, talk with a few before you make a decision. Look for someone who might have brokered deals for companies that are similar to yours, or at least can claim some knowledge of the field and how to interest a prospect in a business like yours.

Business Sale Tip . . .

If for some reason the sale of the business includes your home office or any other property, it pays to make it look as nice as possible, but without going overboard in extensive redecoration. Most who buy property with a business will change it anyway, and as long as things are shipshape and structurally sound, you should be okay.

There are some unique aspects to selling a home-based business. It's likely that you'll be selling the business and perhaps applicable equipment and supplies, without selling any buildings or land. A business broker or your lawyer can guide you through that process.

A business that you've started and grown is personal. You may have developed close relationships with customers, suppliers, employees, and others, and, when trying to sell, it's natural to look for someone interested in maintaining those relationships and proving the same level of quality and service that you have. Here are a few tips that will help you move the right prospect to make the right offer:

- Try to get a number of offers, even if you know that some might not be your "perfect" replacement.
- Get as much information as you can about each before you get into any serious discussions and negotiations; a key factor will be whether or not each is financially qualified to buy your business.
- Once you have several serious contenders, stay in touch with each regularly. Don't be pushy, and don't give the impression that you are anxious to sell. Just hinting that others are thinking about buying the business is enough to keep the more serious prospects in the game.
- Leave yourself some negotiating room. Try to give on lesser points while holding firm to the price you are asking. A few minor concessions can often make the difference without having to lower your price.
- Whenever you and a potential buyer come to terms on a disputed issue, put it in writing immediately, send it to him or her, and ask for a confirmation. Selling a business is a step-by-step process, and the more issues you can

confirm this way, the less likely they are to surface when you are down to the short strokes.

- Selling your business is not like selling your car or some tools you don't use anymore. You are selling something very personal. It's a business that you've built, and, even when you've thought it through and know that selling it is your best option, it can be difficult. Rely on others for help and remember that life goes on after the business is sold.

Frequently Asked Questions

1. *What factors should I keep in mind as I consider whether or not to sell my home-based business and move on to something else?*

   That's a good question, and one that only you really can answer satisfactorily, because nobody else can know exactly how you're feeling about your business and what you think you might like to be doing in the future. In short, however, you should consider: your personal goals, the responsibility you have to your employees and what would happen to them if you were to sell your business, your vendors with whom you've probably spent a lot of time building relationships, any personal circumstances that might affect your decision of whether or not to sell. Deciding whether or not to sell your business is rarely easy. Even entrepreneurs who are looking forward to retirement struggle with what's the right time to sell.

2. *If I decide to sell my business, do I have any options, such as staying on for a while until I find something else?*

   There are all kinds of ways to negotiate a business sale, so it's important that you get some good legal and business advice before moving ahead. You could negotiate to stay on board for a year as a consultant or officer. Maybe you'd want to consider being a limited partner. You might be planning on starting another business that would be a competitor, so that would need to be addressed. Yes, you have options, but you need to explore them carefully and get some sound advice about how to proceed.

3. *My dream is to pass my home-based business down to my kids. How should I begin preparing for that?*

    Passing along your business is a dream for many entrepreneurs. Unfortunately, it can turn out to be a nightmare if circumstances aren't right. First of all, how do you know your kids want the business? Have you had any frank and truthful conversations about it? Businesspeople sometimes assume their children will want to carry on family businesses, when, in actuality, nothing could be further than the truth.

    If your kids do want your business, you've got to be sure they know what they're doing. Insist that they work for another company in the industry first, in order to gain experience and some perspective. After that, have them work within every aspect of your business so that they get to fully understand how it works. Bring them on board as early as possible, having them work in the trenches during high school and college, and then placing them in a position for which they're qualified. If you hand over the business to children who are not properly prepared to run it, you could end up risking both your business and your familial relationships.

Appendix I: Checklist of Start-Up Requirements

This home-based business start-up checklist is from Entrepreneur.com., which offers an extensive and comprehensive Web site to help and guide those starting and running their own businesses. Other checklists for various aspects of running a home business are available on this Entrepreneur.com site: www.entrepreneur.com/encyclopedia/checklists/article81938.html.

Planning Your Business

- Write your business plan and create a schedule for regular updates to it
- Create your marketing plan
- Create a financial plan. Determine if you have enough money to survive for six months while your business gets off the ground. Decide if you need start-up funding

Making Your Business Legal

Business Name

- Have you said it aloud to make sure it's easily understood and pronounced?
- Has it passed muster—including a spelling test—with your family and friends?
- Have you checked the local Yellow Pages and with your local business authority to make sure the name is available?
- Have you started your trademark search?
- Have you filed your DBA?
- Have you registered your trademark?
- Business licensing
- Obtain a city business permit

- Obtain a county permit, if necessary
- Determine whether you need professional licensing from your state
- Inquire as to any other permits you might need, including a fire inspection or sign permit
- Determine the proper amount of sales tax you need to collect and obtain a "seller's permit"

Other Legal Tasks

- Determine if your neighborhood is zoned for home businesses, and if you need to be aware of any regulations (parking, signage, etc.)
- Find an attorney who specializes in small businesses
- Decide which business structure (sole proprietorship, partnership, corporation, limited liability partnership, limited liability company) you desire for your business, and contact your attorney to get the paperwork underway
- If you plan to hire employees, obtain an employer ID from the IRS and any forms you and your employees need to fill out. (Also inquire at your local INS office for an Employment Eligibility Verification form (Form I-9), which proves your employees have the legal right to work in the United States.)

Money

- Get a business bank account
- Buy business accounting software
- Hire an accountant
- Determine your start-up financing needs
- Create a budget

Your Office

- List three places for a potential office, and do a physical inventory of your possibilities:
    Are there easily accessible phone and electrical outlets?
    Will your current desk or table fit in the location?
    Is lighting and ventilation adequate?
    What is the noise factor?
    Is there room to spread out your work?

- If you have inventory, list three possible locations for storage and, again, survey each location:
  Is it climate-controlled? Will you need climate control?
  Is there adequate lighting, ventilation and space for you to easily access your inventory?
  Will you need to construct special shelving or add other storage space?

- Set up an ergonomically correct work space, including a desk, chair, and storage areas
- Decide which technology you need, including a computer, PDA, communication equipment, an office suite of software and computer peripherals like printer, scanner and storage devices
- Outfit the office for visitors if your business requires them. Create a sitting area, and make sure visitors can access it without traipsing through your house
- Make sure your office is safe and secure

Insurance

- Research business insurance, and contact your insurance agent (or find a new one) to add the policies
- Check for fire and safety hazards like loose cords, precariously stacked items, clutter and too many plugs in one outlet
- "Hide" your office from the view of strangers by investing in window covers if it's at the front of the house
- Install a security system
- Create a system for backing up data and storing it offsite

Marketing

- Create a logo and print identity for your marketing materials
- Write a marketing plan
- Build your Web site
- Join networking organizations

Other Sources for Answers to Your Questions about Starting a Home-Based Business

Best Home Business Opportunities
www.gofreelance.com/home-business

Business Week Smart Answers – Starting a Home Business
www.businessweek.com/mediacenter/podcasts/smart_answers/smart_answers_01_20_09.htm

Home Based Business
www.home-based-business-world.com

Home Based Business for Women
www.wwork.com

Home Based Business Resources
www.business.gov/start/home-based

Home Business Center
www.homebusinesscenter.com

Home Business Ideas for Mothers
www.freelancemom.com

Home Business Magazine Online
www.homebusinessmag.com

Home Business Resources
www.usahomebusiness.com

Information to Start and Run A Business
www.atouchofbusiness.com

MSN Money: Top Home Businesses
http://articles.moneycentral.msn.com/Investing/Extra/TopHomeBusinessesList.aspx

North East Veterans Business Resources
www.nevbrc.org

Say Home Business
www.sayhomebusiness.com

Small Business Bible
www.smallbusinessbible.org

Starting a Home Based Business
www.home-based-business-opportunities.com/c-basics

Starting a Home Business
www.startingahomebusiness.org

Starting Your Home Based Business
www.foxbusiness.com/story/personal-finance/on-topic/small-business/help
-starting-home-based-business

The Top 10 Home Based Businesses for Women
www.selfgrowth.com/articles/Top_10_Best_Home-Based_Businesses_for_Women
_to_Run_in_2009.html

The Top 10 Home Based Business Scams
www.scambusters.org/work-at-home.html

The Top 25 Homes Based Business Ideas
www.allbusiness.com/specialty-businesses/home-based-business/3315-1.html

United States Small Business Administration
www.sba.gov

By State
Alabama: Starting a Business and Small Business Resources
www.alabama.gov/portal/secondary.jsp?page=Business_Startinga Business

Business Homepage for the State of Alaska
www.state.ak.us/local/businessHome.html

Arizona Small Business Association
www.asba.com

Arizona Business Department
http://az.gov/webapp/portal/topic.jsp?id=1158

Arkansas Business Overview
http://portal.arkansas.gov/business/Pages/default.aspx

California Small Business Services
www.pd.dgs.ca.gov/smbus/default.htm

Business in Colorado
www.colorado.gov/archive/20080527/colorado-doing-business

Colorado Metro Mart
www.cmmart.com

Connecticut Small Business Resources
www.ct.gov/sots/cwp/view.asp?A=3175&Q=391770

Delaware Business Resources
https://onestop.delaware.gov/osbrlpublic/Home.jsp

Florida Business Resources
Myflorida.com

Georgia Department of Economic Development
www.georgia.org/Pages/default.aspx

Georgia Business Resources
www.ready.ga.gov/Your-Business/Resources-in-Georgia

Hawaii Department of Business, Economic Development and Tourism
http://hawaii.gov/dbedt/business

Hawaii Community Development Authority
http://hcdaweb.org/business-resources

Business Resources for the State of Idaho
http://business.idaho.gov

Idaho Department of Commerce
http://commerce.idaho.gov/business

State of Illinois Business Portal
http://business.illinois.gov

Illinois Business and Consumer Resources
www.bcr-illinois.com

Indiana University Kelley School of Business Research Center
www.ibrc.indiana.edu

Indiana Business and Employment
www.in.gov/business.htm

Indiana Business Builder Homepage
www.indianabusinessbuilder.net

Iowa Small Business Development Center
www.iowasbdc.org

Iowa Department of Business and Economic Development
www.iowa.gov/Business_and_Economic_Development

Network Kansas
www.networkkansas.com

Kansas Business Center
www.kansas.gov/businesscenter

Kentucky Small Business Development Center
www.ksbdc.org/resources

State of Kentucky Business Resources
http://kentucky.gov/business/Pages/default.aspx

Louisiana Business Resources
www.louisiana.gov/Business

Louisiana Small Business Grants
http://usgovinfo.about.com/od/smallbusiness/a/labusiness.htm

Maine Business Resources
www.maine.gov/portal/business

Small and Home Based Business Programs (Maine)
www.umext.maine.edu/Waldo/business

Maryland Department of Business and Economic Development
www.choosemaryland.org

Central Maryland Small Business Development
www.centralmdsbdc.org

Massachusetts Department of Business Development
www.mass.gov

State of Michigan Business Guidebook
www.michigan.gov/som/0,1607,7-192-29943_31466---,00.html

Michigan Local and Small Business Resources
www.mlive.com/business

Twin Cities Business (Minnesota)
www.tcbmag.com

State of Minnesota Business Resources
www.sos.state.mn.us/home/index.asp?page=92

Mississippi Development Authority
www.mississippi.org

Mississippi State Business Resources
www.mississippi.gov/ms_sub_sub_template.jsp?Category_ID=21

Missouri Business Development Program
www.missouribusiness.net

Missouri Department of Economic Development
http://ded.mo.gov

Montana Business Resources Division
http://businessresources.mt.gov

Nebraska Department of Economic Development
www.neded.org/content/view/89/162

Starting a Nebraska Business
http://nbdc.unomaha.edu

Doing Business in Nevada
www.nv.gov/DoingBusiness_nevada.htm

Resources for New Hampshire Business
www.nh.gov/business/index.html

New Hampshire Business Resource Center
www.nheconomy.com

New Jersey Business Portal
www.state.nj.us/njbusiness/index.shtml

New Jersey Business News
www.njbiz.com

New Mexico Small Business Network
www.nmsbdc.org

New Mexico Department of Employment, Business and Economic Growth
www.newmexico.gov/business.php

New York State Small Business Development
www.nylovessmallbiz.com

New York City Entrepreneur Meet Up Group
http://entrepreneur.meetup.com/23

Business Link North Carolina
www.blnc.gov

North Carolina Business Resources
www.n-carolina.com

North Dakota Department of Commerce, Economic Development and Finance
www.business.nd.gov

North Dakota Small Business Development Center
www.ndsbdc.org/resources

Ohio Business Gateway
http://business.ohio.gov

Ohio Department of Development
www.odod.state.oh.us

Oklahoma Business Resources
www.ok.gov/section.php?sec_id=4

Oregon Local and Small Business
www.oregonlive.com/business

Oregon State Guide to Starting a Business
www.oregon.gov/menutopic/business/bus_dev_starting.shtml

Pennsylvania Open For Business
www.paopen4business.state.pa.us

Pennsylvania Small Business and Home Office Resources
www.office1000.org/Pennsylvania

Rhode Island Government Business Resources
www.ri.gov/business

South Carolina Business One Stop
www.scbos.com/default.htm

South Carolina Business Resources
www.scsea.org/resources_business.htm

South Dakota Governor's Office of Economic Development
www.sdreadytowork.com

South Dakota Small Business Development Center
www.usd.edu/sbdc

Tennessee Department of State Business Services
www.tennessee.gov/sos/bus_svc

Official Portal of Texas: Business
www.texasonline.com/portal/tol/en/bus/home

Greater Houston Partnership Business Guide
www.houston.org

The Official Business Web site for the State of Utah
www.utah.gov/business

Utah Business Resource Center
www.utah-business.com

Vermont Department of Economic Development
www.thinkvermont.com

Vermont Official State Web site Business Resources
www.vermont.gov/portal/business/index.php?id=86

Commonwealth of Virginia Business Home Page
www.virginia.gov/cmsportal3/business_4096/index.html

Virginia Department of Business Assistance
www.dba.state.va.us

State of Washington: Doing Business
http://access.wa.gov/business/index.aspx

University Of Washington Business Resources from Foster Business Library
www.lib.washington.edu/business/bizweb

West Virginia Business and Industry
www.wv.gov/business/Pages/default.aspx

West Virginia Chamber of Commerce
www.wvchamber.com

Wisconsin Department of Commerce
www.commerce.state.wi.us

Wisconsin Department of Commerce: Business Development
http://commerce.state.wi.us/BD

Wyoming Business Resources
http://wyoming.gov/business.aspx

Support and Sanity for Entrepreneurs
Atlanta Entrepreneurship Center
www.atlantaeec.com

Appalachian Regional Commission Entrepreneurship Initiative
www.arc.gov/index.do?nodeId=19

Bard Center for Entrepreneurs
http://thunder1.cudenver.edu/bard

Boston Entrepreneurs' Network
www.boston-enet.org

Business Week: Entrepreneurship
www.businessweek.com/smallbiz/running_small_business

Chicagoland Entrepreneurial Center
www.chicagolandec.org

Campus Entrepreneurship
http://campusentrepreneurship.wordpress.com

CONNECT Business in San Diego
www.connect.org

Council for Entrepreneurial Development
www.cednc.org

Dallas/ Fort Worth Entrepreneur Network
www.dfwent.com

DC Entrepreneurs
http://dctechnology.ning.com/group/dcentrepreneursweb20

Disney Entrepreneur Center
www.disneyec.com

Entrepreneur America
www.entrepreneur-america.com

Entrepreneur.com Blog: Up and Running
http://upandrunning.entrepreneur.com/2009/07/01/is-entrepreneurship-declining

Entrepreneur: Business and Small Business
www.entrepreneur.com

Entrepreneurs and Entrepreneurship
entrepreneurs.about.com

Entrepreneur Forum of Greater Philadelphia
www.efgp.org

Entrepreneur's Foundation of Central Texas
www.givetoaustin.org

Entrepreneur's Foundation of North Texas
www.efnt.org/content-about-affiliates.asp?id=35

Entrepreneur's Journey
www.entrepreneurs-journey.com

Entrepreneur Meet-up Groups
entrepreneur.meetup.com

Entrepreneur Ohio: Helping Ohio Businesses
www.entrepreneurohio.org

Entrepreneurs Organization
www.eonetwork.org/Pages/default.aspx

Entrepreneurs and Small Business Information and News
www.forbes.com/entrepreneurs

Entrepreneurship and Ethics
www.gregwatson.com

Entrepreneurship Research and Policy Network
www.ssrn.com/erpn/index.html

Entrepreneurship Worldwide
www.entrepreneurship.org

Fifty Plus Entrepreneur (Small Business Administration)
www.sba.gov/50plusentrepreneur/index.html

Finger Lakes Entrepreneur Forum
www.flef.org

Florida Virtual Entrepreneur Network
www.flvec.com

Fuel for Entrepreneurs
www-rohan.sdsu.edu/dept/emc

Global Entrepreneur Center
www.entrepreneurship.fiu.edu

Global Entrepreneurship Institute
www.gcase.org

Great Lakes Entrepreneur's Quest
http://gleq.org/gleq.nsf/index.html

Indianapolis Enterprise Center
www.indyincubator.com

International Entrepreneurship
www.internationalentrepreneurship.com

International Trade Association: Fostering Entrepreneurship Worldwide
www.entrepreneurship.gov

Iowa Entrepreneur Network
www.iowaentrepreneur.com

iVenture Entrepreneur Network
www.entrepreneur.net

Library of Congress Entrepreneur's Reference Guide
www.loc.gov/rr/business/guide/guide2

Make Your Community Entrepreneur Friendly (Georgia State Gov)
www.georgia.org/BusinessInGeorgia/SmallBusiness/EntrepreneurialCommunities
/Pages/EntrepreneurFriendly.aspx

Memphis Entrepreneurship Institute
www.memphislibrary.org/ftsbc/where/mei1.htm

Minority Business Entrepreneur Magazine Online
www.mbemag.com

MIT Entrepreneurship Center
http://entrepreneurship.mit.edu/outside_orgs.php

MSNBC Business: Entrepreneurs
www.msnbc.msn.com/id/8546545

My CEO Life
http://myceolife.com

Nebraska Entrepreneurs
http://ecedweb.unomaha.edu/entrepreneur/home.htm

Network for Teaching Entrepreneurship
www.nfte.com

Nevada's Center for Entrepreneur and Technology
www.ncet.org

New Jersey Entrepreneur
www.njentrepreneur.com

New Jersey Entrepreneur Forum
www.njef.org

New York City Entrepreneurs Organization
http://eoaccess.eonetwork.org/ny/Pages/default.aspx

Northeast Entrepreneur Fund
www.entrepreneurfund.org

Northwest Entrepreneur Network
www.nwen.org

Oregon Entrepreneurs Network
www.oen.org

Policy Dialogue on Entrepreneurship
www.publicforuminstitute.org/nde

Portland Open Source Software Entrepreneurs
www.possepdx.org

San Jose Entrepreneurial Assistance
www.sjeconomy.com/businessassistance/entrepreneurassistance.asp

SCORE Counselors to America's Small Business
www.score.org/index.html

Seattle Networking For Entrepreneurs, Investors and Venture Capitalists
www.iloveseattle.org/categories.asp?CATEGORYID=5

Small Business and Entrepreneurs
www.hispanicbusiness.com/entrepreneur

Small Business and Entrepreneurship Council
www.sbsc.org/home/index.cfm

Small Business Information for the Entrepreneur
www.inc.com

Small Business Marketing: The Wall Street Journal
http://online.wsj.com/public/page/news-small-business-marketing.html

Start Up Nation: By Entrepreneurs for Entrepreneurs
www.startupnation.com

The Closet Entrepreneur
http://theclosetentrepreneur.com

The Collegiate Entrepreneurs Organization
www.c-e-o.org/page.php?mode=privateview&pageID=124

The Concise Encyclopedia of Economics
www.econlib.org

The Entrepreneur's Help Page
www.tannedfeet.com

The Entrepreneur's Mind
www.benlore.com

The Entrepreneur Network
www.tenonline.org

The Indus Entrepreneurs
www.tie.org

The Kauffman Foundation: Entrepreneurship
www.kauffman.org

The Lester Center for Entrepreneurship and Innovation
http://entrepreneurship.berkeley.edu/main/index.html

The San Francisco Entrepreneur Group
www.meetup.com/changemakers

Upstate South Carolina Entrepreneur Forum
http://upstateforum.org

United States Association for Small Business and Entrepreneurship
http://usasbe.org

U.S. Senate Committee on Small Business and Entrepreneurship
http://sbc.senate.gov

Utah Entrepreneurs
www.uec.utah.edu

Western North Carolina Entrepreneur Organization
www.brecnc.com

Wisconsin Entrepreneur's Network
http://wenportal.org

Women Entrepreneurs
www.womenentrepreneur.com

Women Entrepreneurs of Baltimore
www.webinc.org

Women Entrepreneurs of Oregon
www.oregonweo.org

Young and Student Entrepreneurs
www.youngmoney.com/entrepreneur

Young Entrepreneur
www.youngentrepreneur.com/forum

Index